The media's watching V
Here's a sampling of ou

"Unflinching, fly-on-the-wall reports... No one gets past company propaganda to the nitty-gritty inside dope better than these guys."

— Knight-Ridder newspapers

"Best way to scope out potential employers...Vault.com has sharp insight into corporate culture and hiring practices."

— Yahoo! Internet Life

"Vault.com has become a de facto Internet outsourcer of the corporate grapevine."

— Fortune

"For those hoping to climb the ladder of success, [Vault.com's] insights are priceless."

— Money.com

"Another killer app for the Internet."

— New York Times

"If only the company profiles on the top sites would list the 'real' information... Sites such as Vault.com do this, featuring insights and commentary from employees and industry analysts."

— The Washington Post

"A rich repository of information about the world of work."

— Houston Chronicle

Vault Guide to
Schmoozing

Vault Guide to Schmoozing

Marcy Lerner, Ed Shen, Mark Oldman,
Hussam Hamadeh, Samer Hamadeh

For information about permission to reproduce selections from this book, contact Vault, Inc. P.O. Box 1772, New York, New York 10011-1772, (212) 366-4212.

Library of Congress CIP Data is available.

ISBN 1-58131-205-9

Printed in the United States of America

ACKNOWLEDGEMENTS

Vault would like to acknowledge the support of Matt Doull, Ahmad Al-Khaled, Lee Black, Eric Ober, Hollinger Ventures, Tekbanc, New York City Investment Fund, Globix, Hoover's, Glenn Fischer, Mark Hernandez, Ravi Mhatre, Carter Weiss, Ken Cron, Ed Somekh, Isidore Mayrock, Zahi Khouri, Sana Sabbagh, and other Vault investors, as well as our family and friends.

Portions of the *Vault Guide to Schmoozing* were written by Julie Z. Rosenberg and Douglas Cantor. This book is also the result of the extraordinary efforts of Catherine Cugell, as well as Clarissa Londis, Rob Schipano, Jake Wallace, and the entire Vault design team.

Special thanks to everyone who agreed to do a little schmoozing with us in order to make this book possible.

CONTENTS

INTERVIEWS

RANKINGS

CELEBRITY PROFILES

SCHMOOZING QUOTIENT TEST

CHAPTER 1

INTRODUCTION

What does schmoozing sound like to you? Maybe it sounds smug, unctuous, oily, slimy. It sounds, quite frankly, like 'oozing.' Schmoozing is far from slimy, but 'oozing' actually isn't a bad description of what a schmoozer does. A schmoozer slides into opportunities where none are apparent, developing friendships from the slightest of acquaintances. Through formless, oozy, schmoozy action, a schmoozer moves slowly but inexorably towards his or her goals.

What is schmoozing? Schmoozing is noticing people, connecting with them, keeping in touch with them — and benefiting from relationships with them. Schmoozing is about connecting with people in a mutually productive and pleasurable way — a skill that has taken on new importance in our fragmented, harried, fiber-optic-laced world. Schmoozing is the development of a support system, a web of people you know who you can call, and who can call you, for your mutual benefit and enjoyment. Schmoozing is the art of semi-purposeful conversation: half chatter, half exploration. Schmoozing is neither project nor process. It's a way of life.

How does schmoozing differ from networking? Conventional networking is the clammy science of collecting business cards ad infinitum, of cold-calling near strangers to grill them about possible openings in their places of work and beg them for favors. No one particularly likes to network, and no one likes to receive a call from a desperate, edgy networker either. If you've read some of those networking books and felt uncomfortable about putting their advice into practice, there's a good reason for your reluctance. Networking is awkward, it's artificial, and more often than not, it doesn't work that well.

Schmoozing, on the other hand, is natural and effective. What could be more normal that calling up new friends to let them know the latest news in your job search? Why wouldn't you let it slip to your hairdresser that you're looking for a new apartment? One of the things you'll learn as we profile schmoozers high and low is that, yes, personal contacts are important to their business and (of course) personal lives, but in the end, they are simply following their natural inclinations. They just enjoy meeting and keeping in touch with people.

Can schmoozing help bring you professional success? Of course. Most people at the top of their fields are terrific schmoozers. They understand the importance of maintaining a strong, supportive and diverse circle of contacts to call upon. This book will help you understand and use schmoozing to find a job, schmoozing for career advancement, schmoozing the CEO that just happens to step into the elevator with you. We'll also show you how schmoozing can help you in those non-workplace situations — cocktail parties, airport lounges, laundromats.

We know schmoozing, and we know schmoozers. We at Vault schmoozed with some of the best, both household names and regular folks, to find out just how they do it. Read on, and you'll find out too.

CHAPTER 2

TRUE TALES OF SCHMOOZING SUCCESS

Schmoozing: An overview

They get free meals for making small talk! They nab choice apartments by striking up conversations on planes! They find their jobs through parties that span different coasts and continents! They head Fortune 500 companies because of parties they attend as tagalongs to their significant others!

Strange, but true. These are the true tales of schmoozing success.

Jeremy

In his previous incarnation as a health care consultant in Virginia, Jeremy says, "a good part of my job was schmoozing." During his time there, his firm oversaw a major merger between two hospitals. "In a merger situation, my job as an underling was just to make people feel good about the situation they were in."

These days, as a medical student in Boston, Jeremy is the archetype of the penurious, chronically starving graduate student. Not only is he pursuing a medical degree, but he is about to begin work toward a Ph.D. On the phone with his girlfriend one night, tallying costs with a ballpoint pen and a napkin, Jeremy figured that he wouldn't actually have an income until the year 2007, at which time he would be $186,000 in debt. Food represents a necessary but sometimes troublesome strain on his expenses.

So Jeremy occasionally uses his social skills to snag a free meal. Walking around his medical school campus, he encounters a constant stream of symposia and luncheons meant for alumni, faculty and other professionals — not hungry students.

"I think people often overlook the direct benefits of schmoozing," he explains. "In other words, while many think about what they can gain down the road by being sociable, they overlook what can be gained at that instant."

"For example, I walked by the atrium of the medical school, and found a rather gala assortment of Mediterranean-type food," Jeremy says, noting that the cuisine is "incidentally my favorite type to do this thing with, because it's easy to get a balanced meal in discrete, readily consumable packets."

"It was a conference labeled 'Celebrating 150 Years of Pathology.' I came up with a few stock questions, such as 'So when do you think pathology really began?' or 'What is pathology in your mind, philosophically speaking?' or 'Is this event celebrating 150 years of pathology per se, or as it is practiced at the medical school?'"

"Luckily, after only talking to two or three pathologists, I saw a classmate of mine doing the same thing. We were free to break off and converse as two professionals rightly positioned at the buffet table, chatting about our personal lives."

Marla

Marla (not her real name), a political consultant in Los Angeles, tells the story of finding an apartment through someone she met on an airplane.

She had been stranded at the ski resort in Lake Tahoe, Calif., over a recent New Year's holiday, trying to get to the airport in Reno, Nevada. "The airport was under water. You couldn't get to the airport, [as] all the roads were closed," she remembers. "The one week we went was the one year in 100 they had this flood."

When she finally grabbed a flight, Marla found herself next to another weather-weary traveler. They started chatting about the weather and immediately hit it off. When she learned that the man, Greg, was a real estate broker specializing in Beverly Hills properties, she mentioned that she wanted to move from Westwood to Beverly Hills. She had been looking for an apartment for about a month. Within a week Greg found a choice apartment for her. "Hardwood floors, two bedrooms, washer-dryer," Marla relates. "The building looks like it's a little Italian villa. It's got a lot of character, a lot of charm. It's very uncommon for an apartment in Beverly Hills to come with washer and dryer – it had everything."

As for the standard broker's fee, Marla says it was never discussed. "I didn't ask – [brokers] usually mention it beforehand and he never did. I think it was something he did, in all honesty, because once he found out what I do, he knew he could get referrals from me. He was schmoozing too."

Since their meeting on the plane, Marla and Greg have kept in close touch. "We're great friends," Marla says. "I'm so busy with work, relationships aren't my biggest priority, but I go to a lot of black-tie functions for work, and a lot of social things — premieres and hotel openings — and Greg is a great escort, a great stand-in date." Marla, who always tries to strike up conversations on flights, has no doubt that even their initial personal connection was instrumental to his finding an apartment for her so quickly. Greg, she notes, is not hurting for business – he often sells million dollar homes to Hollywood types.

"I had been looking for a month with two brokers," she says. "I found an apartment within a week with him."

IT'S A MATTER OF LIFE AND DEATH

Can schmoozing save your life? Maybe. In a celebrated study of close to 5,000 Alameda County, Calif. residents that began in 1965 and went on for a decade, researchers found that those who reported the least social contact – whether that contact was romantic, filial, social, even professional – died at almost three times the rate of those who reported the most. In another widely-cited study, begun in 1989 by Stanford Medical School doctor David Spiegel, advanced breast cancer patients participating in weekly support groups were found to have an average survival period nearly twice as long as the women who did not participate. One sociologist has calculated that social isolation is as large a factor in illness and death as smoking.

And when it comes to health and schmoozing, it's not just about mortality, either. Social support and contact are important factors that affect how effectively our body wards off the simplest of ailments. In 1997 researchers at Carnegie Mellon University in Pittsburgh, Pennsylvania, tried shoving it up our noses to prove it. In that project, led by psychologist Sheldon Cohen, 276 people had purified cold viruses sprayed up their noses. Those who reported having the least developed social circles were four times as likely to develop a cold as those at the more social (and apparently, healthier) end of the spectrum. The most interesting aspect of this study is that it measured the effect of having a wide variety of relationships. Subjects were asked to report whether they had frequent contact with people in 12 categories such as spouse, friends, and colleagues. About 35 percent of the people with frequent contact in more than three categories came down with a cold; 62 percent of those with fairly developed relationships in three or fewer categories became sick.

Carl

Carl Bettag, part owner of a 25-person San Francisco-based product design consulting firm, explains that he got his job through a series of parties that spanned New York, London and San Francisco. "Sometimes just being social and lucky can help," he remarks. "Making friends and contacts doesn't have to involve talking about work. Just by enjoying yourself and meeting new people, you automatically increase your chances of learning about a new opportunity or being put in touch with the right person."

"I went to a party in New York with Rich Stanley, a friend from college," says Bettag. "I didn't know anyone but wound up meeting and talking to a group of women designers – after a bunch of beers – who went to Carnegie Mellon University." Bettag was leaving for London; the women gave him the name of one of their friends there.

"I was living in London, looked up Fred and became friends – over lots of beer," he says. "Fred and I both returned to the Bay Area shortly thereafter. I went to a party with Fred and met a bunch of other people from Carnegie Mellon." One of those people was a soon-to-be friend named Gregor, who put Bettag in touch with Bill Evans, the founder of Bridge Design. "No beer, just coffee," Bettag says about his meeting with Evans.

"I have been working at Bridge for five years," Bettag reports, "and was made a part owner of the firm."

"Incidentally," Bettag says, "my wife and I were looking at a place in San Francisco. We decided not to take it and told Gregor about it. He's still living there seven years later. To top it off, David Maltz, one of Bridge's other co-owners, was an old college acquaintance who I met years later over a few glasses of wine at a friend's dinner party and who has been with Bridge ever since."

JOSEPH AS A SCHMOOZER

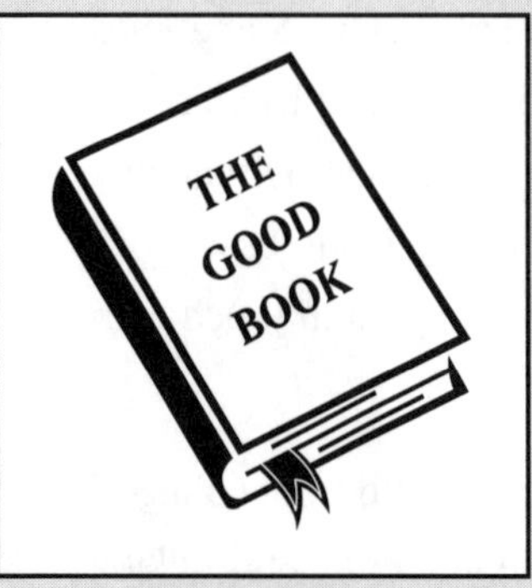

Schmoozing has been around as long as there have been people to be schmoozed. If you look closely, you can find evidence of schmoozing in the Bible itself. The book of Genesis tells the story of Joseph, son of Jacob who (with a little divine assistance) learns how to schmooze the hard way.

The story begins with Joseph, the youngest of 12 sons and his dad's favorite. After Joseph gets a "coat of many colors" (Genesis 37:3) from his father, his brothers are understandably jealous. Joseph is insensitive to his brothers' displeasure – he's not yet a good enough schmoozer to figure out when people are annoyed. Instead, Joseph has a dream where the sun, moon, and 11 stars bow down to him – and he tells his brothers about it! "And his brothers were jealous of him" (Genesis 37:10). *Bad idea! Bragging (even if divinely inspired) is hardly the way to get along with your kith and kin.*

After Joseph's been enslaved, things get worse, although his schmoozing skills improve. Joseph works hard and impresses his master Potiphar. Unfortunately, Potiphar's wife takes an interest in the "handsome and good-looking" (Genesis 39:6) Joseph, and pesters him for sex. Joseph attempts diplomacy, modestly saying he wishes not to offend either Potiphar or God. *(Joseph makes a good attempt at deflecting Potiphar's wife – he doesn't turn her down directly or insult her.)* Ultimately, however, the annoyed spouse frames Joseph for attempted rape, and he is sent to prison.

But it's in prison that Joseph really hones his schmoozing skills. There, he notices that the butler and baker of the king of Egypt (each imprisoned for their own misdemeanors) look troubled. Conversationally, he asks, "Why are your faces downcast today?" (Genesis 40:7) When he learns they've had dreams they can't interpret, he offers to give it a try. *This is good schmoozing behavior – be sensitive to the moods of others, and offer to assist – but don't be pushy.* Joseph predicts that the butler will soon be restored to the Pharaoh's good graces (the baker, sadly, will be executed for his poor milling technique).

Two years later, when the Pharaoh has a dream he can't figure out, the butler remembers the young man in prison who seemed so talented at dream interpretation. Joseph is summoned to court.

Joseph as a Schmoozer, cont'd...

A perfect schmoozing lesson! Good schmoozers offer to help others without knowing when their assistance will pay dividends. If Joseph had sulked in his cell instead of chatting with the butler and the baker, he never would have had the chance to prove himself.

Pharaoh tells Joseph that he's had a dream in which he was "standing on the banks on the Nile, and seven cows, fat and sleek, came up out of the Nile and fed in the reed grass, and seven cows came up after them, poor and very gaunt and thin. And the thin and gaunt cows ate up the first seven cows" (Genesis 41:18). Joseph interprets this dream – there will be seven good years in Egypt, then seven famine years. *But he doesn't stop there – he makes a policy recommendation. Good schmoozers know how to continue a conversation.* "Let Pharaoh select a man discreet and wise," advises Joseph, "and take the fifth part of the produce of the land of Egypt during the seven plenteous years." (Genesis 41:34) That overseer, Joseph continues, would ensure that there would be a reserve through the seven lean years. And who'll oversee this project? Does Joseph make a direct, and possibly alienating, bid for the job? No, he simply suggests that Pharaoh should "select a man discreet and wise, and set him over the land of Egypt" (Genesis 41:33). *A beautifully indirect suggestion! Schmoozers never ask directly for what they want.*

Pharaoh, of course, thinks that Joseph has already shown himself to be discreet and gives him the job. Though Joseph is now in a position of power, he doesn't refrain from helping those below him. In fact, when his brothers travel to Egypt in search of food, he treats them generously, and gets to see his father Jacob before he dies. *Our final lesson: Good schmoozers do not hold grudges; grudges are unproductive.*

Bob

Bob Eaton worked as a janitor and clerk at Montgomery Ward, as a forklift mechanic at a fruit cocktail cannery in California, and as a night superintendent at a pea cannery in Oregon before graduating from college in Kansas. He went to work for GM and gradually worked his way up the corporate ladder, starting with a two-year college graduate training program. He starred in training films as a demonstration driver. He was an executive engineer, then an assistant chief engineer, and then a vice president. In 1988 he became head of GM's European Division. Then in 1992, Bob Eaton crossed over to the other side to become the chairman and CEO of Chrysler, the successor to Lee Iacocca.

Eaton's succession of Iacocca was no sure thing – he leapfrogged over several much more prominent candidates, including top Chrysler officials. The choice of Eaton paid off for the auto giant. In 1997, Chrysler was named Company of the Year by *Fortune*, and Eaton was named Executive of the Year by *Automotive Industries.* Eaton retired in 2000.

But Eaton's climb to the top spot at Chrysler wasn't just the product of years of nose-to-the-grindstone work. According to *Comeback: The Fall and Rise of the American Automobile Industry*, Eaton owes his position largely to a chance meeting at a party decades earlier, and a close relationship that developed out of that party. In the 1960s, Eaton's wife Connie taught grade school in a Detroit suburb with a woman named Margie Hubacker. At a party the two women attended, Connie's husband, Bob, met Margie's husband, Fred, who worked at Chrysler. The two men and the two families struck up a fast friendship. They went out to dinner, rented vacation spots together, and eventually bought vacation condos near each other.

Thirty years later, when Chrysler was looking for a CEO, Hubacker, a middle finance manager at the company, wrote a letter to Iacocca recommending his longtime friend. Iacocca was struck by Hubacker's audacity – by writing the letter, Hubacker risked the ire of upper-level Chrysler officials who were vying for the job. He had Hubacker arrange a meeting with Eaton. After a few months and another personal recommendation letter from Hubacker, Eaton was announced as Iacocca's successor.

Benjamin Franklin

Moral: Combine work and pleasure

Benjamin Franklin, generally considered to be the third most important founding father after Jefferson and Washington, was a politician, diplomat, scientist, journalist, publisher, author, philosopher, teacher, inventor, and schmoozer.

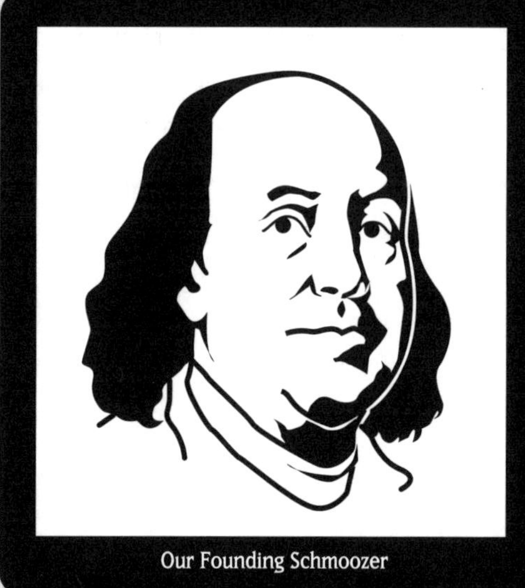

Our Founding Schmoozer

Franklin conducted some of his most important work in Paris, negotiating French-American treaties of friendship, trade, and general alliance – essential to the rebellious colonies' victory against Britain. Franklin achieved this success because he followed another principle of the schmoozer: realize what the other side wants and put the negotiations in that context. As Barbara Oberg, the editor-in-chief of the Franklin Papers told *The New York Times*: "Franklin was enough of a diplomat to realize that the treaties could be attained because they also fit into France's own plans and position in European affairs." Franklin's diplomatic style was said to be smooth, amiable and yielding – as opposed to his American colleague John Adams, a brusque, unfriendly man.

This alone would have been a fabulous schmoozing accomplishment – but Franklin also found time for the ladies during his Paris sojourn. Franklin admitted in his autobiography that he had a "hard-to-be-governed passion that often led him to "intrigues with low women that fell" his way. And boy, did these women fall. Although Franklin went to great lengths to keep quiet his lifelong affairs, his numerous dalliances with the fair sex were well known.

Franklin profile, cont'd...

The elderly Franklin was condemned by the sour John Adams as a "scene of continual discipation."

But just how did Franklin attract all these women? He followed a fundamental principle of the schmoozer: flatter others by showing genuine interest. An associate of Franklin, the London publisher William Strahan, wrote that "women, young and old, loved him because he took a keen interest in them, not merely as objects of desire, but as people with a different outlook, with their own contributions to make. He listened to them, he was not afraid of them – obvious principles of courtship too often lost sight of."

The ever-curious Franklin took an interest in everything, whether it was studying the phenomenon of lightning, founding America's first magazine and post office, ending slavery, gaining independence for America, or flirting with cute French women. Today we remember him as one of America's first great schmoozers.

Test Your Schmoozing Quotient

1. You are on an airplane. The man sitting next to you stares straight ahead. Do you:

a) Hope he doesn't get up too much and scrutinize the in-flight magazine

b) Make a witty comment about the ease of smuggling plastic explosives through X-rays

c) Introduce yourself

d) Smile at him and wait for him to talk to you, if he wants

2. It's December. Who are you mailing holiday cards to?

a) No one — postage costs way too much

b) No one — you only send out St. Patrick's Day cards

c) Your friends and family

d) Everyone in your address book

3. You are looking for a job. What do you do?

a) Ask your mom to get you a job

b) Read the want ads

c) Tell everyone you know that you're looking for a job

d) Find someone in the field and send them your resume

4. You are still looking. At a party, you discover that one of the attendees is the recruiting director at a firm of interest to you. How do you proceed?

a) Approach him and give him your business card

b) Ask the host of the party to introduce you to him so you can get a job

c) Hang around him and hope for an opening to talk

d) Go up to him and ask who he knows at the party

5. On your first day at work, the CEO gets on the elevator with you. You:

a) Introduce yourself and tell her it is your first day on the job

b) Ask her what floor she wants

c) Grill her about the company's Asian strategy

d) Tell her you think she is the unrivaled genius of our century

6. **You are at your office Christmas party. You:**
   a) Fondly reminisce with your office buddies about your first month on the job
   b) Go look for your boss so you can tell him he is a genius
   c) Say hi to the new receptionist and get her a drink
   d) Get a drink so you can relax

7. **Someone tells you to "take a long walk off a short pier." You:**
   a) Giggle over the antiquated insult
   b) Start chatting about the diving awards you won in high school
   c) Direct cuss words at them
   d) Smile pleasantly and walk away

8. **You are in a Brontë sisters chat room. Someone posts an inquiry about finding a hairdresser in New York City. You:**
   a) Hit delete — you live in Chicago
   b) Post a brilliant message about Jane Eyre's changing hairstyle
   c) Send them the e-mail address of your friend, whose sister lives in New York — maybe she knows someone
   d) Post an irate message about the room being spammed with unrelated messages

9. **How often do you speak to your cousins?**
   a) Once in a blue moon — mostly weddings and funerals
   b) Once in a while, when you think of it
   c) You let your parents handle family arrangements
   d) You are close and speak often

10. **Which of the following describes you? (check all that apply)**

a) Curious	b) Cynical	c) Extroverted
d) Quiet	e) Talkative	f) Flirtatious
g) Generous	h) Shy	i) Critical
j) Sensible		

Calculate your score with our explanations on p. 289.

CHAPTER 3

THE SCHMOOZER'S MINDSET

Strangers to friends

Think about somebody you feel comfortable with. Now think back to before you knew this person. That person, that stranger, at one point, didn't exist in your social universe. But now you would feel comfortable asking to stay over if you happen to be in town on business, asking him to pick up dry cleaning for you if you're in a bind, or asking him to help you seek out job opportunities. How strange. At the same time, how normal. The acceptance that everyone is a potential good friend is the first step towards schmoozing success.

Curiosity compelled the schmoozer

There are many ways that strangers become acquainted – they work together, they share a train ride, they bump into each other at the corner deli. But regardless of the way people meet, one thing has to happen for that gossamer thin, yet seemingly indelible, line that separates friends from strangers to be broken: one person has to talk to the other.

While there are situations when we are required to talk to others – at work, to order food, to get somebody to move in a crowded mall – what differentiates the schmoozers from the mere mortals is that they enjoy striking up conversations when they don't have to. And when they find themselves in a routine conversation, they are willing to take the conversations further than is required.

The schmoozer sees opportunity where others see strangers. A schmoozer is curious.

WHY AMERICA LOVES SCHMOOZERS

Ever since the Pilgrims sat down with the American Indians for a feast, America has been a land of schmoozers. Although it is unlikely that John Smith exchanged business cards with Pocahontas, they still made a connection that led to new and exciting opportunities — and even inspired a movie several centuries later. The Pilgrims and American Indians took a chance meeting each other for a meal, but that's the point: you never know what kind of wonderful things will happen unless you get rid of your fears and prejudices and start connecting.

Taking chances is what America is all about. From Lewis and Clark to Armstrong and Aldrin, Americans have sought to boldly go where no one has gone before. Although schmoozers may not have to climb mountains, cross raging rapids, or risk burning up in the atmosphere, schmoozing captures the pioneering spirit of America too. Through schmoozing you meet new people who will introduce you to more new people, and so on and so forth. You never know where schmoozing will lead you – but that's the point.

There is something else about schmoozing that America loves: the way schmoozing levels hierarchy. Schmoozing connects the passenger and the driver, the businessman and the busboy, the CEO and the mail clerk. Why is *Huckleberry Finn* generally considered the Great American Novel? Well, among other reasons, it shows how schmoozing can eliminate the artificial barriers of society. At heart, the novel is about the relationship that forms between a boy and a runaway slave, and the adventure that results.

Americans love to even the playing field. Schmoozing plays into the American belief that this is a land of opportunity where anyone can make it, regardless of meager beginnings or initial lack of connections. America has had a soft spot for the underdog ever since the first shots were fired in Lexington and Concord. Just think of the popularity of Horatio Alger's rags-to-riches stories, the 1980 U.S. Olympic ice hockey team, and *The Little Engine That Could.* America has always pulled for the guy or gal or train that fought the odds.

So next time you're at that cocktail party where you know no one and have an urge to leave, remember: America is rooting for you to stay, to introduce yourself to other guests, to find surprising things in common, to make friends, to find hidden opportunities. America is rooting for you to schmooze.

Although curiosity is to some extent inborn, it can also be cultivated – or rather, rediscovered. In *The Beast in the Nursery,* popular British psychotherapist and author Adam Phillips argues that psychoanalysis is primarily an attempt to treat failures of curiosity. The mission of many patients undergoing psychoanalysis, he says, is to reactivate the intense curiosity of childhood.

While most of us do not suffer from overwhelming ennui that drives us to the therapist's couch, we can all relate to a waning of curiosity. We become accustomed to our modes of living, calcified in our modes of thought, fearful or derisive of newness. After the first few months in a new apartment, we lose the zeal to redecorate.

While all of us are familiar with this narrowing of curiosity through our experience, recent research suggests that this sad fact has a neurological basis: aging contracts our neural networks and makes thought processes more repetitive. Artists, scientists and other thinkers seem to lose their creativity as they grow older. It's why Einstein had trouble accepting that God would play dice with the universe – and why the Stones just don't make albums like they used to.

At the same time, Phillips' belief that failures of curiosity can be treated has a sound neurological basis. University of California at Berkeley neuroscientist Marian Diamond has shown that stimulation can increase the number of brain cells in adults – albeit adult rats. And in 1997 similar research at the Salk Institute in La Jolla, Calif. showed that mice placed in a stimulating environment that included a varied diet and regularly changed bedding learned mazes much more quickly than mice whose environment did not change. (University educators, take note.) Most impressively, the environmentally stimulated mice had, on average, 15 percent more brain cells.

Although human brains are normally much more complex than those of rodents, neuroscientists agree that the experiments have relevance to the capacity of the human mind to continue expanding. Dean Keith Simonton, a psychologist at the University of California at Davis, has discovered that the ebbing of creativity is not dependent on chronological age, but on how long a person has been working in his or her field. Scientists who change specialties often show a burst of creativity and energy.

In his study of "flow," an optimal state of concentration and enjoyment, Dr. Mihaly Csikszentmihalyi (try remembering that name at a cocktail party) has found that people are most alert and happy when demands on them are slightly greater than normal, and a bit more is required of them. His work (which some consider to be revolutionary because it emphasizes improving life, rather than treating disorder) stresses that "flow" can be found through any activity – from chess to painting to chopping food. (Athletes commonly refer to the state as "being in the zone.")

Harvard psychologist Ellen Langer believes this state of "flow" can be entered through simply paying active attention to seemingly routine aspects of life, a state she calls "mindfulness" — simply paying attention to details and opening oneself to small changes.

The best schmoozing is done in these states of mindfulness and flow. It's easy to sink into routine life. Let's face it, it's comfortable. Most of us do the same things and talk to the same people day in and day out. Even when we're not happy, we cling to the same routines, because we're used to them. Curiosity can make the difference between "blah" and "flow."

As a start to boosting your own curiosity, try making small changes in your routine. Take a different route to work. And when you do, look around and notice the differences. Key in on anything unusual – maybe a tree you haven't seen before. Look at its leaves, examine its roots.

Try the ginger beef instead of the sesame chicken you have every time you get Chinese. If you notice a different coffee shop, make a point to drop in; don't avoid it because you don't normally go there. Maybe change your bedding once in a while. Flannel vs. satin – it can make a difference.

And then, say hi to someone. Stretch your social sphere. It's a whole new world.

Overcoming shyness

Sure, one may be curious, you say, but curiosity may also be directed at balls of yarn and other unthreatening inanimate objects, rather than the unpredictable world of people. Of course, you may say, it's less unnerving to focus on a safe, immobile tree than on a living, breathing, constantly changing human. If so, you're not alone. According to a 1996 *Psychology Today* survey, close to half of all Americans describe themselves as shy. (Shyness was defined for the survey as being excessively self-conscious in public and when meeting strangers.)

But like curiosity deficits, shyness can be overcome with practice. Winston Churchill, one of the great speechmakers of the 20th century, supposedly passed out the first time he addressed Parliament.

Behavior is self-reinforcing. A schmoozer becomes more comfortable with people by schmoozing – just as shy people have their reticence confirmed by their lack of interaction with others. According to the *Psychology Today* survey, the incidence of shyness among Americans has risen about 10 percent since 1987, in part because we don't interact with people as often. Experts believe the the proliferation of contact-avoidance tools, such as touch-tone movie schedules and automatic teller machines, have made us a shyer, less schmoozy society.

THE OVERLY SHY

Jonathan Berent, a psychotherapist with a practice in Great Neck, New York, has specialized in treating shyness for the last 15 years. Berent tells the story of a patient named Arthur, who came to him as a 17-year-old. "He didn't go to school, because he had social anxiety," Berent says. "He had school phobia." As a teenager, Arthur had no friends and was depressed and suicidal. Through group therapy, Berent says, Arthur has confronted and faced down his anxieties. He is now is working toward a Ph.D. and is living with a girlfriend, Berent reports. Berent has taken Arthur on programs such as the Oprah Winfrey and Jenny Jones talk shows as a testament to the ability to overcome shyness. "This kid couldn't go to school, and now he's appeared on national TV with me," Berent tells us. "

Psychologist Bernardo Carducci, who co-authored the landmark 1996 *Psychology Today* survey that showed that almost half of all Americans identify themselves as shy, says that shyness runs across gender, industry and class — playing no favorites in deciding whom to skip (except for some differences among cultural backgrounds). Because of the prominence he has achieved since the *Psychology Today* survey, Carducci receives a great deal of mail from the shy world. "I get letters from people all over the world – if you'd read them, they'd break your heart," he says. "They're about the pains of shyness. Eighty percent of them end with 'Help me.'"

The author of *Overcoming Shyness* (1993, Simon & Schuster), Berent believes that while people are in part genetically predisposed to be either timid or gregarious, the timid often use genetics as a crutch to shield themselves from confronting their fears. Ultimately, he says, the only way the shy will overcome their fears is to confront them. He emphasizes that this should be done with support. This safety net often comes in the form of support groups. But for those who are so shy that even a support group seems daunting, the support can come in the form of a trusting relationship with a therapist, Berent explains.

While most of the people who identify themselves as shy aren't afflicted with anxiety to the extent that Arthur was and may not feel the need for group therapy sessions, Berent's practice is still not only inspirational but informative. If the key to overcoming shyness is to find ways to move into social situations that provide a built-in support structure, what we should do is identify those situations.

The Overly Shy, cont'd...

Carducci, who is working on a book called *The Shy Life*, suggests volunteering as a way to develop social skills in a non-threatening, non-judgmental atmosphere. Forcing yourself to go to a bar and talk to people when you don't feel comfortable can be ineffective and harmful if it's outside your comfort zone, he says. Another type of support structure Carducci believes can help is a "central theme"; he suggests that the schmoozing-challenged attend events like art gallery openings or poetry readings. "Events with central themes are useful because the central theme gives you a hook," Carducci says. "It gives you something on which to build a conversation."

For those who make it out to parties but find themselves hesitant to mingle, Carducci suggests providing a "social grace" by getting a drink or serving food, or performing some other function. "By offering a social grace, that takes the pressure off of you," he tells us. "It takes the focus away from you. For shy people, the biggest problem is there's an excessive amount of social consciousness."

Carducci, who grew up in a big Italian family that provided "lots of chances to practice social skills," says he doesn't treat shyness as something to be overcome. Instead, he simply tries to present options that help people make "informed decisions."

"You can stay home or you can volunteer," he says. "You can stay by yourself at a party, or you can provide a social grace, offer to do something."

As a first step to breaking the circle of shyness, approach strangers with the simplest of requests. When you have questions – about things ranging from what that thing on the wall is, to what's in the dish you're eating – seek out answers from those around you. Even if their answers may not be as authoritative as those in encyclopedias or computers, they flavor your life with elements of human interaction, and allow you to practice the art of conversation. (See inset for expert tips on combating shyness.)

HRA Poster

Don't worry. Be optimistic.

If success in life and love were solely based on academic ability and intellectual prowess, there would be no need to schmooze. But we all know that this isn't the case. That's why Daniel Goleman's book *Emotional Intelligence* hit such a nerve when it was published in 1995.

In the much-celebrated book, Goleman argues that emotional skills are also a form of intelligence and predict career success much more accurately than conventional I.Q. measures. The book put into words what seems intuitively obvious: the ability to deal with people is crucial to managing one's life and career. Fortunately, identifying and encouraging the traits exhibited by high Emotional Quotient (E.Q.) people can raise both our own E.Q. and, by extension, our schmoozing quotient.

Understanding optimism, for example, can help us counter shyness. Goleman explains that everyone encounters setbacks in life, but those with high E.Q. view these setbacks as temporary or singular occurrences – and simply move on. Low E.Q. people, on the other hand, take these setbacks as signs that they will not succeed in life and brood obsessively about their inevitable failure. Understandably, this isn't a recipe for successful human interaction.

To back up this analysis of the importance of optimism, Goleman cites a classic survey of door-to-door salespeople, performed by Martin Seligman, a psychologist at the University of Pennsylvania. In a study of MetLife insurance salespeople, optimistic salespeople sold 37 percent more insurance than pessimists did. Seligman then persuaded MetLife to hire a group of applicants who tested highly as optimists. These bright-eyed sales professionals sold 21 percent more than pessimists their first year and 57 percent more their second year on the job. Understanding the role optimism plays in this type of study is easy: pessimists reported being despondent and personally slighted after having the proverbial (and literal) door slammed in their face. Optimists simply moved on to the next door, viewing rejections as temporary setbacks. Sooner or later, those happy, high-E.Q. salespeople found customers with whom they forged profitable connections.

It's called teamwork

Even if you're curious and outgoing, you may have a different obstacle looming on the road to schmoozing success: schadenfreude, the tendency to gain pleasure from another's misfortune. (Literally translated from German, it means "bad joy.") Sound like something sinister reserved for the likes of Lex Luthor, the Penguin and other arch villains? Far from it. It was psychoanalysis guru Sigmund Freud who theorized that all humor has to do with a sense of superiority. We find it funny when a character in a sitcom walks into a wall, because that person feels pain and we do not. And Charles Darwin's "survival of the fittest" theory implies that we might instinctively rejoice when one of our rivals falls off the evolutionary ladder.

If we are honest with ourselves, most of us can remember instances of feeling schadenfreude – when a co-worker has been taken to task for a mistake, when someone obviously uncomfortable in a social setting stands alone while others (like ourselves) chatter away amiably.

Schmoozers sidestep these tendencies toward schadenfreude and envy. While we still strive to be successful, we cease seeing success as a zero sum game. We choose instead to follow a strategy of helping one another, believing that helping others will help us.

THOSE FUNKY MONKEYS

Is the "jungle" a bad term to use when talking about ultra-competitive, better-watch-your-back environments? Maybe. Consider the bonobos.

An endangered species of primate that lives in the Congo, bonobos are the species (along with chimpanzees) most closely related to humans – they share more than 98 percent of their DNA with us. Bonobos were not identified as a species distinct from chimps until 1929 (they are also known as pygmy chimpanzees). Although they are about the same size as chimps, they have black rather than brown faces.

Chimps and bonobos are considered "cousins" to humans; both branches derive from a common ancestor in a split that took place 6 million years ago. While chimpanzees, especially male chimps, are aggressive and hot-tempered, bonobos are sensitive and lively. When it comes to gender roles, bonobos are also more egalitarian than chimps. In chimp social groups, each male is ranked higher than the highest female. In bonobo hierarchy, the highest-ranking male and highest-ranking female have the same status, the second highest-ranking male and second highest-ranking female are on the same level, and so on. And while chimpanzees exhibit aggression when facing outside groups, bonobos in the same situation defuse tension with veritable orgies that involve rump-rubbing, kissing, genital touching, and sex. Bonobos, the only animal other than humans known to French-kiss, use these frenzied sexual rituals when confronted with the need to divide food, meet strangers, or to alleviate boredom – and have a relatively peaceful society to show for it.

Of course, initiating rump-rubbing at cocktail parties and trade conventions may not be the way to schmooze to success. But understanding that affiliative, or cooperative, behavior is often the natural state is a start to overcoming the schadenfreude that often holds us back from developing potentially fruitful relationships. Frans de Waal, a renowned chimpwatcher at the Yerkes Regional Primate Center at Emory University in Georgia, has devoted much of his career to exploring the naturally affiliative relations of animals. "Each and every individual has a stake in the quality of the social environment on which its survival depends," De Waal writes in his book *Good Natured.* De Waal describes some pretty compelling examples: a group of elephants leaned into a herd member that had been shot by a poacher in an attempt to hold her up; a group of female chimpanzees pried open the hands of males ready to fight and took away sticks and rocks meant to be used as weapons. And in 1996, Binti Jua, a gorilla at a zoo near Chicago, scrambled into a moat to get a baby that had fallen into her pen and then delivered the child to attendants waiting at her door.

Hogwash, you say, it's a dog-eat-dog world out there, a jungle, every man for himself. Nonsense. The view of human interaction as strictly competitive is as outmoded as the terms "hogwash," "every man for himself," and all those other clichés in that first sentence. The model of cooperative social interaction, scientists are discovering, has a strong biological basis. Now a new generation of sociobiologists has begun proposing a kinder, gentler evolutionary world (see inset on the previous page).

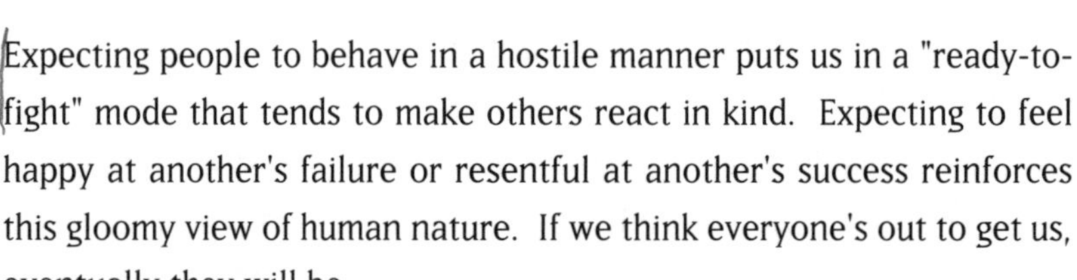

But this is not just a matter of biology; it's a matter of mindset. Knowing that we're not necessarily wired to compete viciously with each other is the first part of overcoming schadenfreude. The schmoozer also understands that putting aside questions of morality, schadenfreude is simply disadvantageous. Those brief moments of bitter joy at someone's failure can't begin to compensate for the opportunities missed through such a sour, uncooperative point of view.

Expecting people to behave in a hostile manner puts us in a "ready-to-fight" mode that tends to make others react in kind. Expecting to feel happy at another's failure or resentful at another's success reinforces this gloomy view of human nature. If we think everyone's out to get us, eventually they will be.

Here's a tip. Don't go into job seeking or apartment hunting, or life in general, on automatic competitive mode. It'll only serve to make others on guard in their relations with you and cut off possible avenues of human relations. When that co-worker gets chewed out by the boss, don't gloat because it wasn't you, take the opportunity to commiserate. When that person stands in the corner alone at the party, don't revel selfishly in your social connectedness – share it. You'll have enough competition out there without being surly with the people you meet. And even more important, if you help people toward success, or even express happiness about their success, their success becomes, in part, yours. A rising tide floats all boats. It's called teamwork.

Social first

What does the word "networker" bring to mind? Most likely, you conjure up an image of someone in a suit, brandishing a business card, pestering you for a time when you can "touch base." It's clear the networker wants nothing from you but the bigger, better job lead or business opportunity. Will you ever see the networker again after helping her out? Don't count on it – unless she needs another favor!

The schmoozer isn't just focused on what he or she can gain and does not explicitly ask for favors (we'll discuss these specific techniques in-depth in the next chapter). While a schmoozer keeps his or her eyes and ears open for opportunity, socialization is the primary goal. This approach holds several advantages. For starters, it puts others at ease. And just as importantly, it puts the potential schmoozer at ease, too. You're not extracting job leads or looking for investors into your new company – you're just chatting and letting them know what you're up to.

Carl Bettag, our job finder from "True Tales of Schmoozing Success," is a good example of the social first principle. "I'm totally casual," he says. "Maybe that's what makes it effective, because people don't feel like I'm trying to network. It's not really intended to be just professional. It's easy. These are just my friends. It's not a burden, it's not like, 'Oh, I need to call so-and-so.'"

Vault Profile: Sid Lipsey

"My father always drilled into me that grades didn't matter, but getting along with people did," says Sid Lipsey, an executive producer at CNN Headline News in Atlanta. "And I've always sought out situations where I needed to work with people. When I was in school, I joined the drama group and the *Declaration*, a student publication. Working together towards a deadline draws people together, and you can make some good friends that way."

This is CNN... Headline Schmooze

Lipsey's penchant for meeting people served him well during a short internship at CNN's Washington, D.C. bureau, which he did during his senior year at the University of Virginia. "I met three people there. Two of them worked in the library, but they knew everything about the company and offered to look for internal job postings if necessary." While Lipsey didn't need to ask the two for any favors, he says he still keeps in touch and "visits with them whenever I'm in D.C." The third person Lipsey met was a human resources employee who advised him on the application process for entry-level jobs at CNN Headline News — where he landed a job as an assistant writer out of school.

Lipsey comments that it's been his experience that "most people you work with are friendly and want to help you. When someone asks you to come to them with any questions, most people don't take advantage of that offer. I always have."

Lipsey profile, cont'd...

As an executive producer at Headline News, Lipsey maintains his optimism when it comes to meeting people. "I would say I like most people I meet," he says. "When I meet people I like, I make sure I give them my story, and say something like 'I enjoyed talking to you, let's get together.' I give them my e-mail, since even a shy person will e-mail you." At work, Lipsey retains his positive view of human nature. "Even if someone is having a bad day – and at a place like Headline News, people do get stressed out – I just assume it's atypical of their normal behavior. Even when someone is consistently rude, I still joke around with them. It never serves you well to be 100 percent mean to someone, even if they deserve it."

Lipsey does recognize that schmoozing has been useful in his career. "You can't convince me that interpersonal relations have nothing to do with success." When chatting with others, Lipsey recognizes that "sometimes in the back of my head I think they could be of help. But I always talk to people because I think they are genuinely nice." He returns the favor as well. "I always try to help people," Lipsey told us. "When people fall through the cracks, I feel awful. I always try to at least point to people who can help someone, if I can't help myself." Summing up, Lipsey says, "I look at it all as a matter of wanting to stay in touch with people whose company I've enjoyed, and to have them in my life."

Unlike the networker, the schmoozer does not direct his or her energies toward a single goal. This is not to say that the schmoozer is not focused. Schmoozers are focused on what is placed before them. While chatting with a potential business contact, if the conversation turns to fly-fishing, the schmoozer talks about fly-fishing.

Curious and optimistic, the schmoozer knows that something good will come of any conversation he or she has. Even if the schmoozer doesn't directly profit, the schmoozer may have made a new friend, or at least learned how to catch a fish. Then, in the future, if fly-fishing once again rears its piscine head as a subject of conversation, the schmoozer may be able to recommend a good trout stream in Montana. And who knows where amiable fishing conversations may turn?

KEY CONCEPTS

- Be curious and try new things.
- Find supportive environments to help overcome shyness.
- Overcome schadenfreude.
- Be social first.

Casanova

Moral: You can become famous through charm.

Giovanni Giacomo Casanova, born in Venice in 1725, was a sickly child plagued by chronic nosebleeds. The son of actors (a lowly profession at the time), Casanova was emotionally neglected in his formative years by parents who worried he would soon die of his ailments. It was only after a supposed magical healing by a witch doctor that Casanova was cured of his condition, after which he flowered into the adventurer and lover we know him as today.

The schmooze of love

Casanova had, according to his own estimate, around 122 lovers, and nearly as many careers. During the first 50 years of his life Casanova's resume included jobs such as: mining inspector in Poland, industrial spy in England, concert violinist, stockbroker, abortionist, silk printer, novelist, priest, soldier, and editor of a theatrical journal. Casanova was also the founder of the Parisian lottery, a translator of *The Iliad* and a proposed reformer of the Gregorian calendar.

Giacomo spent most of his life wandering around Europe on a quest for fortune and pleasure. Traveling from Paris to Rome, London to Prague, St. Petersburg to Madrid, he often stayed in a place just long enough to be chased out again. Casanova's famous escape from prison in Venice, where he was being held by the Inquisition on charges of blasphemy for an anti-clerical poem, was the subject of one of his first books.

Casanova profile, cont'd...

Though of limited means and a humble background, the notorious Casanova was the prized guest of the rich and powerful for much of his life. Casanova's company was highly valued due to his wide knowledge of topics and his wealth of life experience, which, in combination with his considerable charisma, made him a great source of home entertainment in a time without televisions.

Casanova's lovers included wives, schoolgirls, noblewomen, chambermaids, a ballerina, a nun, and one Neapolitan woman whom he planned to marry before discovering she was actually his illegitimate daughter. Oops! Casanova's ability to attract so many lovers is largely attributed to the fact that, despite the misogyny his sexual consumption suggests, Casanova was utterly respectful and in awe of the women with whom he was involved. His entire concern was for their pleasure, their experience. Instead of being presented with an individual who wanted something from them, the women saw in Casanova someone who wanted something for them, as individuals. Hence, historians say, his impressive record of love.

CHAPTER 4

SCHMOOZING 101: THE BUILDING BLOCKS

Welcome to the schmoozing world

Enough already about monkeys and cancer studies and Joseph, you say. Tell me how to schmooze. In this chapter, we will begin to talk about the actual practice of schmoozing. We'll get tips from people in the schmooziest of professions. Fundraisers will tell us how they glad-hand potential donors. Politicians will tell us what techniques they use to make voters think they're sincerely interested when out stumping. Brokers will tell us why their clients trust them with their money. Literary agents and film producers will tell us about "doing lunch." Salespeople will tell us how they lay on their schmoozy schtick. And airline ticket agents and flight attendants will tell us how to deal with difficult people.

Some of the people we'll meet have particular expertise in certain areas of schmoozing, and will give advice in other chapters. But they all have something to say about the rudiments of schmoozing: building rapport.

Although we went over the basics of the schmoozer's mindset last chapter, in this chapter we'll start with more specific tips on how to put yourself in the right frame of mind to schmooze.

Your mission – you should choose to accept it

If you're like many people, you may be shaking your head right now. Perhaps you're among that 40 to 50 percent of Americans who consider themselves shy. Perhaps you can't imagine yourself actually starting a conversation with someone you don't know in a public place or inviting an acquaintance to breakfast.

One thing that helps get the wheels of schmoozing turning is being a man or woman on a mission. Although schmoozing is most fun — and often most effective — without being pointed toward a specific target, having a goal in mind offers an impetus for social interaction. Craig Enenstein, a consultant at Knowledge Universe (see profile on p. 89), Michael Milken's education publishing investment firm in Los Angeles, states it simply: "You have to have a goal, whether that's to own your own business, get a new apartment, or meet people who also enjoy gardening and swing dancing."

"If you don't have any purpose to life, there's no way anyone can give you one," Enenstein says. "It will be harder for people to talk to you."

Your mission doesn't have to be as overarching as "becoming a partner in a San Francisco law firm" or "having my first novel published next year." You might simply decide your mission for the week is to find someone who works at a major accounting firm, so you can discuss a possible career change. Or you might be thinking of taking ice skating lessons and want to learn more about the hobby. A mission gives you a reason to schmooze. Not every schmoozing session or conversation will bring you closer to achieving your mission, but it's good practice regardless. Your mission may simply be to "schmooze more!"

And remember, the subject's the thing. You must believe in what you want in order for your schmoozing to be at all worthwhile. Says Shemilla Subance, a sales representative at HKM, a New York production company that produces commercials and music videos, "You have to believe in your product. If they have something, and your directors are talented, it's not going to sound phony." Granville Toogood, a consultant in Connecticut who has counseled executives on their communications skills at Fortune 500 companies (see profile on p. 223), suggests that "when you're talking, you should try very hard not to worry about how you're doing – concentrate on the value of the message. Don't worry about how you're doing, or you'll get flustered."

Confidence – if you don't have it, how to get it

Even with a mission, some potential schmoozers lack faith in themselves. Will I be bothering people? What do I have to contribute to others? Even with the best of intentions, some people will hesitate before making the final step and approaching someone to schmooze.

There are some easy steps to take that can help you build your confidence. The first: fake it. Schmoozing pros say that even if you don't feel confident, you should simply pretend to be. More importantly, starting with the appearance of confidence, as we will see, can actually bring you greater confidence. This might seem ridiculous, but it's far from it. After all, we fool ourselves all the time — witness the "placebo effect," a term used to describe the improvement of a patient's condition spurred by the mere belief that their treatment will be effective (see inset).

MIND OVER MATTER

By most estimates, about a third of the control patients in a drug trial who receive a dummy pill instead of the real treatment experience an improvement in their condition. In one case, almost 7,000 asthma, ulcer and herpes patients in La Jolla, Calif. were given treatments later found to be (pharmacologically) ineffective. Amazingly, 70 percent of the patients reported getting better.

So how do you build confidence? Start with a smile. A simple smile is a sign of confidence that can help you and your schmoozees feel at ease. In fact, research shows that smiling can positively affect your mood and the mood of the person you are speaking to. In humans, the muscles of the face are connected to the emotional centers of the brain — frowning actually sends signals to your brain that cause you to be unhappy.

In both humans and other animals, facial expressions, like yawning, can be contagious. Frowning can put the people you're with into a funk; smiling can affect them positively — and make everyone's schmoozing experience enjoyable. Try to smile in a way that involves your entire face — smiling just with your mouth (without using the muscles around the eyes) looks forced. When you look at someone you don't know well (or not at all), imagine you are speaking to a friend or close family member. Tell yourself that the person is interesting and that you like them very much. *Then* smile at them.

Faking it works with verbal schmoozing, too. As a former director for the cosmetics company Mary Kay, Bridgett Bailee of San Antonio trained recruits for multi-level marketing. She advised her Mary Kay consultant trainees to pretend they are someone whose poise, speaking and social skills they admire. "I tell them it's just acting, it's not you," Bailee says. "After a while, you forget to act. It's just you."

Acting will also embolden you when it comes to schmoozing for contacts for a specific goal. Lara Rosenthal, an Internet producer and freelance writer (see profile on p. 203), says she has actually feigned interest in a field or hobby just to see where such a conversation can potentially lead. "Something I've tried is pretending my goal is something totally out there, like being a trapeze artist," she says. "People make the most surprising connections, like telling you about someone they know who works with Cirque du Soleil [a renowned circus] or that they teach gymnastics." Once you realize how easy it is, you simply start talking about your real interests. Even if someone has no idea how to help you with your mission, Rosenthal says, "it's interesting, and they will have gotten a little bit of an idea about who you are."

WHAT IF YOU'RE REALLY STUCK?

Sometimes, if we're overworked, stressed or unhappy, it's easy to forget who we are or what we have to contribute. Not only can a lack of confidence make us wary of approaching strangers, but stress and anxiety can make us feel too hurried to meet new people or even to contact the people we know. If you're this stressed, it's fine to step back and take some simple re-energizing measures.

A first step is calling your pals. Ask them: What do you like about me? What do you think is most interesting about me? What kind of impression did you get of me when we met for the first time? You might hear some interesting answers, and you'll be reminded that yes, others will find you worthwhile and engaging.

There are other simple things that can get you in schmoozing mode. Exercise, for one. In the National Health and Nutrition Examination Survey, members of a 2,000-person study group who did not exercise regularly reported a depression rate three times higher than regular exercisers. A study at Duke University showed that workouts can also have a positive effect on mood immediately. Compiling the data from questionnaires given to 55 people who walked as fast as possible on a treadmill for 15 minutes, the researchers concluded that after exercising, the group's feelings of depression, tension, anger, and confusion dropped, on average, 82 percent after the workout.

Massage, according to some studies, has a remarkable impact on both mental and physical health. A University of Miami School of Medicine project called the Touch Research Institute (TRI) has found that massage can be linked to the alleviation of a surprising variety of medical conditions – from asthma and arthritis to diabetes and sickle cell anemia. More important for our schmoozing purposes is the research TRI has performed regarding emotional states. In one study, bulimic adolescent girls showed improved body image, decreased anxiety and stress hormones, and increased serotonin (the feel-good hormone) after regular massage. Workers given a 15-minute massage were shown to have decreased anxiety levels when compared to those who simply rested during the break.

But scientific study aside, common sense tells us that if you've been denying yourself the little things that make you happy, you quite simply won't be as good a schmoozer. People are most attractive and interesting when they are involved in something that they find fascinating. Even if your favorite hobby doesn't provide obvious opportunities to meet and mingle (writing a novel, growing herbs in your backyard), by feeding your soul and indulging yourself, you make yourself a much happier, mentally enriched person – exactly the sort of person others want to meet and schmooze.

These tips should help you build your confidence. But most important, we should remember what we learned from "The Schmoozer's Mindset." To be confident, you should view schmoozing incidents as episodes, or chapters, in that thing called your life — not representative of its major theme. That way, setbacks are not nearly as disheartening. "We have 45 investors but I've been rejected by 450 people," says Andrew Weinreich, the founder of sixdegrees.com, a now defunct company that brought people together online (see profile on p. 126). "I just keep going to people. When they say 'No thank you, go away,' I say, 'Thanks, and we'll let you know when we've hit our next milestone.' One of our investors said no three times. The fourth time, he invested. Now he's our CFO."

"Don't be afraid of failure," Weinreich says. "Try to succeed, but understand that failure, too, is part of the plan. Failure is not that bad."

Recognize your blinders

Many of us still suffer from a hangover from our high school or family upbringing. There was "your crowd" of people, and then there was everyone else. Or maybe you still, consciously or unconsciously, feel uncomfortable around people of different age groups, ethnicities or social backgrounds. Anyone you screen out as too intimidating or alien to schmooze is a loss — yours and theirs.

For some, an ability and willingness to move outside one's normal circles of influence comes naturally. Says Internet CEO Kaleil Isaza Tuzman, (see profile on p. 181) who grew up in Colombia and later lived in Mexico City and India, "I was kind of taught to be interested in different experiences. It helps to be less entrenched with any one group of people."

Dealing with Difficult People

"If you don't have patience, it's not the industry to get into," says Dianna Stauss, an airline ticket agent for Continental Airlines in the Dallas-Fort Worth airport. We all know how it works – the stale air, long lines, elusive baggage, and stress of airports brings out the worst in us.

"I've had people spit. I've had them tear their tickets up and call me the worst names," Stauss says. Why? "Because their flight is delayed because of weather, and because I just can't help that there is a storm outside ... I just sit there and say, I'm sorry you feel that way ... We have a saying at the ticket counter that we always tell each other: 'A hundred years from now it won't matter.'"

The airline employees that we spoke to say that although their companies train them for the inevitable run-ins with irate customers, being able to deal with such situations basically comes down to personal patience and humor.

"The airlines tell you to smile and be happy," says Suzanne Turk, a flight attendant with Atlantic Southeast Airlines. "I do that anyway, but I also try to make a joke out of the situation. You just let the customers be the way they want to be. I'll just kind of smile and laugh at them. I'll just say, 'If you're not good, you don't get any peanuts and pretzels.'"

"They just say handle it as best as possible," says Stauss, who went through a three-day training course before starting as an agent with Continental. "And remember that we represent the company." However, Dianna says there is one important thing her airline provides – the knowledge that it will give her the benefit of the doubt when it comes to customer complaints.

Still, even though airline employees are trained to remain accommodating even in the face of curses or spit, this doesn't mean they never resort to civil honesty.

"We had a passenger that called me and he hadn't even flown on our airline," says Stauss, recalling a lost luggage incident that occurred when she was working for Atlantic Southeast Airlines in Corpus Christi, Texas. "He had reservations, his flight was delayed – and we put him over to American. American handled him the whole time, but he would just call every five minutes saying 'You did this.' He said, 'You are hiding my bags in the back.' I said 'Fine, I'll help you find the bag, just to prove to you that I didn't hide it.' He said, 'I'm going to press charges I said, 'Go ahead, I invite it.'"

"He kept getting worse and worse, and finally I said, 'Sir, there are only two people who give a damn where your bags are, and one of us is losing interest.'"

For others, it sometimes takes a surprising meeting to begin tearing off the blinders. Claire Wilson, a born-and-bred New Yorker, relates the following story. "I was at the wedding of a friend, and his cousin, who lives in South Carolina, had brought his girlfriend Joanna. Well, she was basically your Southern stereotype, at least as I saw it — obviously dyed and permed blond hair, lots and lots of eyeshadow, pink blush in streaks on her cheeks, white patent pumps, and she was wearing this frilly pastel outfit. I figured I would have nothing to say to her."

"It turned out she was both really nice and very smart and fun – she was a lawyer in Charleston," Wilson says. "Afterwards, I realized that my prejudice had almost prevented me from meeting a great new person. I thought because I was from New York I was really open-minded – if Joanna had dyed her hair purple and pierced her tongue, that would have been cool with me — but it turned out I was wrong."

So don't let your misconceptions keep you trapped. Deliberately approach people outside your comfort zone, and you'll often find them just as responsive as anyone else. Schmoozing success soon enters a feedback loop – the more success you have with a wide variety of people, the easier it will seem. Soon you'll see that everyone can be schmoozed.

Enjoy!

Schmoozing is fun. Period. The most important thing to realize is that you shouldn't schmooze others if you're not enjoying it. Don't schmooze with people you don't like. One superb schmoozer, Marla (our apartment finder from "True Tales of Schmoozing Success"), flatly states, "If I don't like someone, I won't schmooze them, no matter how helpful they might be to me." "It's no good if you don't enjoy it," concurs

New York writer Lara Rosenthal.

Even in the ultra-schmoozy entertainment industry, following your instinct when it comes to making connections is the best way to build a support system. "You always hear 'Oh, go to this person, talk to this person,' but I usually find that I'm the best judge," says Beth Calabro, formerly an in-house producer at Miramax films.

"I think the best people in the business are the people who love movies," says Calabro, who notes that she has met many people who do not love movies, but rather are in the industry for its glamour and money. "I think that one of the most important rules in the film industry is not trying to meet everybody, but trying to find people who are good at what they do and who you like. Through those relationships you will do well. I see so many people who try to meet everybody. You just need to meet the right people for you and you will benefit."

Now that you're in the right frame of mind to schmooze, you're ready for the next steps.

Presentation

Presenting oneself for the first time is basically a matter of not messing things up too much. First of all, understand that some non-verbal gestures can be distracting. Covering your mouth (in American culture) is said to be a sign of insincerity. Playing with your hair can be either flirtatious or juvenile, neither of which are impressions you likely want to make. Slouching indicates a lack of interest; so does fidgeting.

But more important, make sure that you pay attention to your basic

MIND YOUR MANNERS

Whether you blame it on Howard Stern or the baby boomers, Americans generally agree that manners (good ones) have declined precipitously in the United States. A 1996 *U.S. News and World Report* survey, conducted in conjunction with the advertising agency Bozell Worldwide, indicated that most Americans feel people have become dangerously rude. Nine out of 10 people surveyed thought incivility was a serious problem; half thought it was extremely serious. Eighty-five percent think rudeness is tearing asunder the very social fabric of the country.

appearance. "First impressions are important, and this is going to sound superficial, but you've got to be well-groomed whether it's in politics or it's interviewing for that job," says Tom Bucci, formerly the mayor of Bridgeport, Connecticut (see profile on p. 217). "That first visual impression is important."

Pay attention

It's easy to zone out when you're introduced to the 30th person that day at the conference you're attending, or to ignore that guy sitting next to you at your cousin's wedding. You may think yourself accomplished simply because you introduce yourself and say hello. But that's just the first step any good schmoozer takes. Where many wannabe schmoozing pros lose their edge is in the follow-up — remembering not only the name of the person they spoke to, but actual details of the conversation.

If you're daunted at the thought of remembering names, spouses' names, kids' names, number and type of pets (and their names too), you're not alone. An entire cottage industry has sprung up around mnemonics, the secret of memory (see inset on p. 57).

Part of the memory problem is that, like shyness, it's self-defeating.

A GUY WITH A GREAT MEMORY

Ed Harper is a full-service investment broker for Prudential Bache in West Virginia. Through his 20-plus years in the brokerage business, he says he has learned that he must bring a personal touch to the broker-investor relationship, or his clients will leave for discount brokers. "I always tell the younger folks, that what they must understand is that the biggest difference between you and Charles Schwab and you and Fidelity – it's the biggest advantage you have – is that they will never call you. Charles Schwab will never call you, but you will call the client. You can't put a price on that, but I think that's a tremendous edge and advantage."

Part of being an attentive broker, Harper says, is paying attention to the details of clients' financial lives. "Not only does the value come in good investment advice, but it's the follow-up servicing," he says. "It's the attention to the little things. It's not just an investment portfolio, it's the retirement account – it's the interest that you need to take with that person's financial well being. It's the kids' college education accounts. Along with that comes the trust and the expectation of not only providing good sound investment advice, but advice with other money matters such as car loans."

And how is Harper so attentive? He remembers. Harper believes that one of the best ways to show that he adds value is to bring up details from previous conversations. "It's all listening. I just park things in my mind," he says.

"With some accounts, I can remember the first stocks a person bought 20 years ago. It helps me with my actively trading clients. I'll say, 'Do you recall when you said if this stock drops to this level, give me a call?' They'll say, 'You know, I forgot about that, you remember that?'" Harper says. "I try to key in on what may be small, and what may seem like insignificant details. You call that person, and they'll say, 'You remember that?' They'll appreciate the interest that you took in that account. Many times, they're just flabbergasted that you can remember it."

People who tell themselves that they can't remember people's names, or that they have a poor visual memory, will probably not listen or observe when they are introduced to someone new – why bother, after all, if you're not going to remember?

Why bother? Because there are simple steps that can improve the recall of even the most absentminded. The most important aid to memory is concentration. When you are introduced, or introduce yourself, to someone new, listen carefully to his or her name. Repeat it to yourself. If it's somehow unclear, ask him to repeat it.

If there's something unusual about the name, ask for its origin or spelling. This will do wonders to help you remember the name, because it will give you a side story or fact — "I was named for the castle my German ancestors lived in," for example — to which you can attach the name. Also, it simply lengthens the amount of time you spend thinking about the person's name to, say, 10 seconds, from the normal split-second. (Even if a person's name seems straightforward, like John or Jennifer, you can say something like "Do you spell your name with an 'H'? or "Are you ever called Jenny?")

After you've learned somebody's name, use it in conversation. If you believe your mind to be especially sieve-like, use the name fairly early in a conversation, before you forget it. Not only will using a person's name help you remember it, but people love hearing their own names, so you will also build rapport.

Because most people think in pictures, not words, it's common to remember someone's face but forget their name. Nonetheless, you should try to fix your schmoozee's physical appearance in your head. Examine their appearance and voice. Do they have an accent? Is there something unusual about their physical features – green eyes, lopsided lips, ringlets?

GINGKO BILOBA TO THE RESCUE

Okay, you've just worked the room, been introduced to all the movers and shakers too, and baby, you know you were looking smooth, passing your card while giving two-fisted handshakes and a flash of your patented smile. Bask in your glory, you deserve it. Go get a drink and join the largest discussion in the room. Display your earnest listening skills and killer wit to the awestruck audience.

But then, 20 minutes later, your buddy shows up fresh-faced with his "Sorry, traffic" line. That's okay, but the first thing the guy blurts out when he joins your little cocktail clique is, "Hey, aren't you going to introduce me to everyone?"

Well, aren't you? What's the matter? Why do you look more confused than Ronald Reagan in his second term? Say something! Oh God. You don't remember anyone's name, do you? Not the lady who invited you to her beach house, not the guy who asked you if you'd ever consider jumping firms, not even that man who confessed to you for an hour about the infidelity of his wife. Now everybody's looking at you, even your dopey friend who's smiling because he has no idea what's going on. How could you forget their names? All of them, so fast? What's wrong with you – are you stupid?

Well, maybe not. Studies show that memory decreases like sex drive: the older you get, the less you've got. Memory functions like a muscle, and many of us have some pretty flabby recall. In addition to the threat of major neurological ailments like Alzheimer's and vascular dementia, most of us are plagued by a simple inability to remember little things, like names. The problem is obvious, so what's the cure?

One popular method of memory improvement is the mnemonics technique. Mnemonics, which gets its name from the Greek goddess of memory, Mnemosyne, is the practice of improving memory through word association and connections. By creating visual links for words and information (e.g., instead of trying to remember that a street is called Tiemann, you remember the image of a man wearing a massive tie). This method, however, is often scoffed at by neurologists, who brush off mnemonics as little more than a parlor trick. Instead, they suggest, those worried about keeping their brain would be better off exercising their minds by picking up a book or tackling a crossword puzzle, abstaining from passive, mentally numbing habits like television.

Gingko Biloba to the Rescue, cont'd...

Many nutritionists say the path to a better memory is simple: just eat more fruits and vegetables. They say that a healthy salad is the key to a solid mind, but experts in other fields warn that there is no concrete evidence to support that approach. And it should be noted that nutritionists give that same answer to just about everything.

As far as effective medications, there have been some recent advances after years of frustrations. Both the drugs tracine and donepezil have been cleared by the FDA for treatment in memory loss, though the focus of their application has been on treatment for Alzheimer's disease. Less expensive is the popular herbal cure, gingko biloba.

Used by the Chinese as a treatment for blood clotting, asthma, and memory loss for the last 5,000 years, gingko works by relaxing blood vessels and reducing inflammation, thereby increasing blood flow to the brain. Though all seem to agree that gingko is to some degree beneficial to the mind, finding real gingko is another matter. Because the FDA does not regulate vitamins, making sure you're buying the actual product, in the proper dosage, is not as easy as reaching for any gingko-labeled bottle on the health store shelf. Your best bet is to stick with the major brands – pay the extra bucks for the proven European brands. Maybe then you can retain something in that noggin for more than a minute, tough guy.

The most common mnemonic trick is to imagine some kind of homophonic representation of the person's name that you can connect to an unusual feature of his or her appearance. For example, if you meet a woman named Madeline with red hair (and you've read your Proust), you might imagine a French pastry sitting on top of Madeline's titian locks. Mnemonics experts swear that the next time you meet Madeline, you'll remember her name, not think of dessert. (At the same time, don't focus too much on changeable features, like dress or hair. If Madeline goes blonde, you might have trouble recognizing her later.)

Now that you're sure you'll remember your schmoozee's name and face, don't let your attention flag. When the object of your attention mentions that his son Adam has just been accepted to Georgetown, or that she's just taking up golf, your job is to remember these facts, as if the person in front of you is the most important person in the world.

If you're just getting your memory up to speed, you may want to take notes. However, you should not let the person you are meeting see you doing this. Just as you wouldn't tell someone named Rick you're remembering him by imagining a raccoon biting his arm, you shouldn't jot down someone's personal details in front of them. After you turn away, you can take your notes.

Bill Clinton, for years, kept index cards on which he catalogued information about the people he met. Other politicians follow suit. "I walk around with 3-by-5 cards, and I'll keep notes, after I've finished talking to them," says Jim, the school board head in a Connecticut town. "Sometimes I wait until I'm in my car. Then I'll go home and enter all that information into my computer database."

Do your research

While remembering is great, anticipating is even better. Ever wonder why some hosts are always in demand, or why some politicians are such wonderful fundraisers? That's because they've discovered the schmoozing power of doing their homework. When you're meeting someone for the first time, it always helps to have done as much of the legwork as possible. If it turns out that you two went to the same school, you can bring that up (see the section later in this chapter on finding similarity). If you're taking the time to learn something about someone, it shows.

Juliet Gumbs (see profile, p. 166), a New York City fundraiser, says that she always prepares for the day when the person who controls the purse strings at a foundation or a potential large donor visits the organization she represents: "You get as much information as possible.

You pick up the phone, talk to other development professionals. 'Is this person no-nonsense, very brusque, or is this a person who is very relaxed, likes to laugh?' One of the reasons you reach out is so you have these resources to draw on."

Victoria Sanders, a literary agent in New York, says she does similar legwork when preparing for meetings with editors at publishing companies. When Sanders opened her own agency in the early 1990s, after having worked at a few major agencies, she sent out letters to "every editor that I could think of ... I got a lot of phone calls from people inviting me to lunch, wanting to meet me. Maybe 10 percent responded, which believe me, kept me busy for a month."

Sanders says that in those meetings, and meetings these days, she asks around to find out about editors. "Definitely if somebody else has had lunch with them, you might ask, 'What do you know about them? Do they work hard?'"

Sanders doesn't do this just to know how to approach an editor, but also to improve her chances of building rapport. "I might say, 'Are they married, do they have children?'" she says. "At some point when you're having lunch with somebody, you run out of business things to talk about."

Vault Profile: Elizabeth Dole

Moral: Form mutual alliances with (or marry) those as connected as yourself (or hopefully more connected than yourself).

Seated on the rear of the doomed gray horse that was Bob Dole's 1996 presidential bid shone a bright red suit and a constant smile that defied the inevitable November gloom. Elizabeth Dole, Bob Dole's wife of 21 years, was a constant ray of sunshine in a campaign with many rainy days. The assistant to President Reagan, member of the Federal Trade Commission, Secretary of Transportation, and Secretary of Labor, Elizabeth "Liddy" Dole has run for president herself and was on the shortlist for President George Bush's possible veep spot in 1988.

Elizabeth Hanford was born in the small town of Salisbury, NC, in the same house her family has occupied since pre-Revolutionary days. Liddy always recognized the importance of an immaculate appearance. Reportedly, in grade school she even painted her glasses with airplane paint so they would match her outfits. In high school, she was teased (perhaps prophetically) that she would be the first female president and was voted by her peers most likely to succeed.

Liddy attended Duke University where her winning charm and ability to schmooze won her the presidency of the student government as well as the May Queen title. After graduation she attended Harvard Law, one of 24 women in a class of 550. During law school the young beauty would hide from suitors, choosing instead to study in the guestroom of the law librarian's house. After completing her degree, Elizabeth left for Washington, where she used her Harvard prestige and connections to land her a job at the White House Office of Consumer Affairs. From there, she moved through the ranks until a fateful business meeting in which she found herself sitting across from the newly divorced and ever virile Senator Bob Dole. Three personal calls later and the Senator asked her out. Three years after that and the romance bill was made a law. Elizabeth and Bob were married Dec. 6, 1975.

Dole profile, cont'd...

The marriage was, in addition to being the union of two very ambitious and passionate individuals, a major career boost for both parties. Elizabeth Dole became even more connected among the Washington elite, as her newfound power and connections led to a position in President Reagan's public liaison office. Once within the White House walls, Elizabeth's long hours and hard work led to her appointment as the Secretary of Transportation, making Dole the only woman in the Reagan cabinet and establishing her as a national figure.

What Bob Dole gained from this marriage was no less tangible. During the last moments of his presidential bid, when he was 20 points down in the polls and it seemed clear that the stiff and awkward candidate couldn't do it alone, Liddy came to the rescue. Hitting the floor of the Republican national convention with an Oprah-esque flair, a technicolor outfit, a bright smile, and a cordless mike in hand, Elizabeth Dole brought sexiness to an unarousing candidate. In the end, Elizabeth's effort may not have won her husband the race, but it did prevent an embarrassing landslide of Mondalian proportions while solidifying her friendly, charismatic image.

How Liddy does it

A former employee of the Red Cross tells Vault how Liddy does it. "Elizabeth Dole is the best schmoozer I know. She's absolutely incredible. What she does is she approaches everybody, smiles warmly and stares straight at them and thanks them, personally, for coming out. She makes so much money for the Red Cross. She's really a tiny lady, but she looks a lot bigger because of her presence, until you see her standing right next to you."

"Wherever she goes, Dole has PR in the city she's visiting do extensive research on each and every person that's going to be at every event she's going to. She wants to know what their hobbies are. If their wife just had surgery, she wants to know that. She wants to know something on everybody there. Even if there's a hundred people at an event, she wants a full dossier on them. She reads over the notes on the plane."

"Then she shows up and says "Joe (or whomever), thanks for coming here tonight. It's great to see you again. (Sometimes she says that even when they haven't met her before.) How's the fly fishing? I was sorry to hear about your father's recent passing," and they think, "Geez, she really cares, I'm going to give her some money." She also tries to find out if they've given to the Red Cross before, if they have employees or factories in a disaster area, or whatever. That gives her a way to touch base with people and get them to give money. If there isn't a direct connection, she just appeals to their desire for good PR."

Take an interest

One of the most distinguishing differences between networking from schmoozing is that schmoozing works only if you take a genuine interest in people. It's fun. You're trying to get in conversations. While you may have a mission in mind, it doesn't matter so much if you achieve your goals or not. People can tell when someone is taking a real interest in them, or when someone is just trying to get another business card in their collection. And people *are* interesting, if you treat them as potential friends and not as networking targets from which to extract information.

J. Owen Todd (see profile on p. 142), a veteran trial lawyer in Boston and renowned schmoozer, says that showing interest is an integral part of building relationships: "I think you have to be able to communicate interest, sincere interest. People can detect when you're asking a question just to be polite, or when you are indeed interested." He says he has learned the importance of taking an interest partly from gauging the responses of juries and witnesses in the courtroom. "You see this when interrogating witnesses, if you're interested in what they have to say, if you sound interested," he says. "It doesn't work if you're asking perfunctorily, as if you already know the answers."

In schmoozefests such as parties, trade shows, or reunions, taking an interest means showing the person that you're talking with that you're focused on them alone. This is a first principle of politicians out campaigning and is one of the many schmoozy attributes attributed to former president Clinton. "If you're smiling or making eye contact with someone while handing a flyer to someone else – that person you're talking with unconsciously knows that you really didn't care about what they had to say," says Jim, our local school board president. "You've got to decide that you're going to do one person at a time."

Schmoozing on the Phone

"Cold calling is probably the single most feared and dreaded thing in the business," says Ed Harper, a full-service investment broker with Prudential Bache securities in West Virginia. Harper understates a bit when he explains that "for most people it's against their nature to call somebody they don't know and try to get them to give you their money." But take heart: "You get better at it as you go on. If you don't get better at it, unless you're a motivated person naturally, you're probably going to have problems."

In our rush-rush age of efficiency, FedExes and satellite offices, we have problems if we can't use the phone effectively. We may not have to make hundreds of cold calls a day, but sooner or later, we'll probably have to make an important call that may be relatively cold, whether that call involves calling up a potential mentor or making a pitch for the company we're starting. We asked some professional phone schmoozers — a stockbroker, a literary agent, and a sales representative — to give us some advice.

"You tell them what you're doing, but first you ask if they might be busy, if there might be a better time," says Harper. "You say: 'This is so-and-so from here and here, do you have a moment to talk?'" *This is the first important lesson of schmoozing on the phone. Just imagine if the other person has someone in his or her office, and here's some schmo yakking like there's no tomorrow.* It sounds like a simple and obvious step, but unless you consciously check yourself, you can fall into it, propelled by nervousness or aggressiveness. "I always ask if they have time to talk," Harper says. "One of the big mistakes people make, is, they'll introduce themselves, say, 'I'd like to interest you in this idea' and they're off and running. There could be someone at their desk, and [the broker] doesn't even realize the prospect can't talk."

So say the person you're calling is willing to listen. What next? On-the-phone schmoozing is a lot like in-person schmoozing. As a literary agent, Victoria Sanders often pitches projects to editors over the phone in a matter of 30 seconds. "You have to have a really hot and snappy pitch," she says. "The biggest thing is you've got to be able to give them a hook. The first question you have to ask is who's the market, who's going to buy it. You've got to help them sell this to the marketing people, because if they won't take it, it won't get sold. In major houses, it's about marketing."

Still, Sanders says that even in a short and intense pitch, one should try to build rapport outside a strictly professional relationship, and that if things go well or a relationship has already been

Schmoozing on the Phone, cont'd...

established, a pitch call can be five to 10 minutes. "It depends on your relationship with the editor. A lot of it's schmoozing – you talk about other things, and then you get to the pitch, or you talk about the pitch and you talk about the other things. It's all about personal relationships."

Sanders' comments point to the fact that even in a brief conversation, we can apply the major tenets of schmoozing that we are learning in this chapter. By concentrating on a "hook," Sanders is concentrating on what the relationship means to the other person — in this case, the editor. By making chitchat outside of the business talk, Sanders is applying the "social first" part of the schmoozer's mindset.

Shemilla Subance, a sales representative with a New York production company, says she will make as many as 120 calls a day and averages somewhere in the area of 100 a day. "You talk to people all day long on the phone," she says. "You talk to producers, directors, copywriters, advertising agencies — the whole gamut."

"You don't want to be boring and cold, you want to be engaging and happy and light," says Subance. However, Subance says that even if one can't see the person on the other line, a good sales rep will be able to mirror him or her anyway and may choose to tone down the pitch. "One moment you might be talking to someone who's a little older, you can tell by the intonations in their voice. You respond accordingly." *A schmoozer is sensitive to his conversation partner.*

A good phone schmoozer, like any good schmoozer, will slide into the situation without being too forward. "The first time I call someone, I don't ever attempt to sell them anything. It's a matter of introduction," stockbroker Harper says.

However, Harper admits to doing a little bit of manipulation of the conversation in order to set up a potential sale. "What I try to do, I try to stay away from a very quick definitive yes or no. I try not to give them the opportunity to say 'No,' on the first question. I don't call someone and say, 'Are you interested in stocks?'" Instead, Harper says, he may ask potential clients on the other line to describe how satisfied they are with their current stock portfolios. *A schmoozer does not set narrow limits.* As a counterpart to the strategy of asking open-ended questions that will not bring a quick end to the conversation, Harper says he also tries to throw questions out that will yield positive responses. "I want to keep the simple yes's coming. Hopefully, that will give me the opportunity to contact them again." *A schmoozer builds rapport.*

Former mayor Tom Bucci says one of the rules he learned while a politician is to stick with voters as long as it takes when campaigning door to door. "You try to limit it to under 10 minutes, but some people would drag you into their house, and you'd blow the night, but you have to do it, because you don't want to insult them. The main thing is not to make a bad impression." If you are schmoozing a group of people, one bad impression can ruin your chances. These situations pop up more often than you might realize. Think about associates trying to make partner at law firms, or even students rushing a sorority or fraternity.

Taking an interest and being patient will eventually pay dividends. "If one night, you talk to 10 to 15 people, the word spreads throughout the neighborhood. It develops its own momentum," Bucci says. "You want a discussion to go to the next level. You want them to talk to your friends the next day. It's going to occur only if you've made a good impression."

Listen up!

Don't think of schmoozing as just talking. The very best schmoozers are superior listeners. Listening is different from hearing or just waiting for your turn to talk. Listening is a skill that takes practice. If you listen to people, you'll better understand how to talk to them and what they want.

Studies have shown that, on average, people retain only 25 percent of what they have heard over the past few days. "It's ironic," says Kathryn Dindia (see inset on p. 69), a professor of interpersonal communication at the University of Wisconsin at Milwaukee. "The communication we do most is listening, then speaking, then reading, then writing. It's the opposite of what we learn in grade school — write and read, and perhaps to speak, but never to listen. There are many poor listeners out there."

Scientists say part of the problem is the very wiring of our brains. While we speak at a rate of roughly 125 words per minute, our brains are able to assimilate speech at a rate of upwards of 500 words per minute. But instead of using this ability to concentrate fiercely on the words of our conversation partners, we tend instead to drift off into the ether, wondering who that cute guy across the room is, or contemplating the evening's menu.

Another problem is that it's simply more fun to speak. By talking, you get your point across, right? Listening, by comparison, seems passive, akin to an insignificant barnacle clinging to the prow of the talker. Wrong! Some of the best communicators are the ones who listen the most. "If you go to a party and ask a lot of questions and just listen," says Wicke Chambers, a communications consultant in Atlanta, "then everyone goes home and thinks you're brilliant. Listening is the best way to connect with people."

How to become a pro listener? "Ask a lot of questions first," advises Jim, a Connecticut school board head Vault interviewed. "Then shut up and listen. Try to figure out who they are. Concentrate." Jim says that one technique he has picked up through years of campaigning is to repeat a comment a voter has made, rephrased as a question so that it is clear he is interested and listening: "If you say, 'What's important to me is that people wear blue shirts,' I may rephrase that and say, 'Well, I know you think it's important that people wear blue shirts — but why?'"

Wicke Chambers suggests that you treat each conversation like an interview. "Try to find out interesting things about the person," she says. "When you ask a good question," advises Chambers, "never sit around in knots thinking of the next question you need to ask. Take a mini-vacation. Sit back and breathe. Don't crowd people and don't be afraid of a little bit of silence. That allows people to compose their thoughts."

THE PROFESSIONAL LISTENER

Kathryn Dindia, a professor of interpersonal communication at the University of Wisconsin at Milwaukee, says there are ways people can show they're really listenting. "There are a few things we can do to show we are paying attention," says Dindia. "Good listeners are listening even while they are speaking. They are paying attention to the non-verbal signals of others."

- Make eye contact. "Studies have shown that listeners make more eye contact than speakers," says Dindia. "If you don't make eye contact, the person speaking will be unsure whether or not you're hearing them."
- Smile. "You'd be surprised how many people forget to smile," Dindia comments. "That doesn't mean you should sit there with a smile pasted on your face, but you should react once in a while."
- Make appropriate gestures. By leaning forward, toward your conversation partner, and nodding, you show that you are listening and understanding. "Even when we can't hear what someone is saying, we often nod anyway, just to show our participation in the conversation," says Dindia.
- Provide what Dindia calls "minimal responses." These include both non-verbal gestures like nodding and smiling, and voiced responses such as laughing and saying "Oh, really?"
- Ask targeted follow-up questions that show you've understood and assimilated what you've been told.

Breaking these rules gives the impression that you aren't listening and don't care. Dindia advises against interrupting the speaker – "that shows you're just waiting for a chance to speak, instead of paying attention." And asking questions or making comments that don't follow naturally from what the speaker has just said are also off-putting – Dindia terms them "irrelevant responses." Perhaps most important, not reacting or making eye contact also conveys disinterest. What if non-verbal cues you give don't match your words? "Ninety percent of the time, people will believe their eyes, not their ears."

Follow-up questions are key – they show you've actually listened to what's been said. "If you listen," comments Chambers, "you'll almost always learn some interesting crumb of information that you can comment on and store away. People will be happy to answer your follow-up questions – they want to know that you understand what they want. And everyone will tell you what they want if you listen closely."

Find similarities

Why do people glom together in groups, from alumni associations, to fraternities, to quilting clubs? People instinctively gravitate to people they have something in common with, and will, in fact, like them better as a result. That's why people bond so strongly during summer camp or the first year of college, when everybody is coping with the same experiences, and why even weak affiliations will induce someone to speak to you or to help you.

Car salesmen, for example, are often trained to look for evidence of background and interests while examining the customer's trade-in car. If they find tennis rackets, for example, they might comment on their desire to hit the courts that weekend. If they see a shopping bag from a nearby department store, asking about the store (where they shop frequently) might work. One researcher found that customers were more likely to buy insurance from salespeople who matched them in age, religion, political persuasion, and even cigarette-smoking habits.

Jim, the school board head in Connecticut, explains how he introduced himself when first campaigning for a position on the board. "I'd say 'Hi, I'm running for the Board of Ed, and the reason I'm doing it is, I have two kids," he says. "You find common ground."

What this all means is that if you show some trait or opinion in common with someone you're speaking with, they will be inclined to like you better. The power of similarity is such that it can even work by proxy as well. If someone has a kid about your age, you may remind them of their child and make them feel positively about you before you open your mouth. Beth Anrig, the owner of a career placement service in Connecticut, recalls helping a recent client above and beyond her normal services. "He was about the same age as my godson, had the same educational background, even resembled him a bit. I just liked the kid."

Once you understand the importance of similarity and likeness, you can start to understand how curiosity, taking an interest, and finding similarities should be integrated into a schmoozing strategy of finding out about lots of stuff. Before she was a fundraiser, Juliet Gumbs was an anthropologist — she studied archaeology in Mexico and Native Americans in the Dakotas. Her wide range of interests provides her with ample ammunition when braving the social world of fundraising. "It helps to be a little eclectic in your interests and contacts," she says. "I'm that way because I'm nosy. Any sort of knowledge that you have that intersects with another person's world is good. The more you know, the more interested you can be in them."

And then it's your job to establish these connections of similarity, no matter how tenuous they might seem. Talk about having visited Virginia if the other person grew up there; mention that your cousin is an attorney if the other person is too.

Vault Interview: George Plimpton, Author

The editor of the influential literary magazine The Paris Review, *George Plimpton has lived a life more varied than the Baskin-Robbins flavor list. As a cub reporter, Plimpton barely hobbled off the mound after pitching two unsuccessful innings to an all-star cast of baseball legends like Willie Mays and Hank Aaron (although he did get Mays to pop out). In the ring, Plimpton went toe to toe with the light-heavyweight boxing champion Archie Moore, who left him bleeding on the canvas. On stage he braved the howls of the crowd for Amateur Night at the Apollo. His varied experiences have brought him to the lightest of comedic situations and to the heaviest of real-life tragedies. He hosted the 100th episode of the pointedly farcical* Married With Children; *in 1968, while covering the Democratic primaries, he helped wrestle assassin Sirhan Sirhan to the ground as Bobby Kennedy lay dying. Most recently he played a psychiatrist in the Oscar-winning film* Good Will Hunting, *completed a biography of social maven and writer Truman Capote, and published a collection of writing from the* Paris Review.

"The Man Who Knows Everyone"

During his 40-year career, this real-life Forrest Gump has managed to work his way into a myriad of different worlds, schmoozing with everyone from Muhammad Ali to Truman Capote and earning the reputation as "the man who knows everyone." Who is the best schmoozer that "the man who knows everyone" has ever known? Vault decided to ask him.

Vault: You seem to be comfortable with a wide variety of people: athletes, musicians and presidents. What accounts for your bravery? Have you always been good with people?

Plimpton: I think so, yes. My father was a lawyer who entertained a lot, so the house was always full of people. We were taught to join in with the adults as much as we could. So we weren't banished to the back of the house when company was there.

Vault: So from an early age, you were brought out?

Plimpton: From an early age, yes. Not brought out, but forced out ... I grew up in a time when the men always would go to one room and smoke cigars. I can always remember sitting and listening to them talk.

Vault: Have you ever been intimidated by anyone?

Plimpton: Of course.

Vault: How do you deal with that, when you need to work with someone, call someone, or speak to someone when your heart is pounding and you're not sure?

Plimpton: You just push your way through it. I don't know that there are any keys. My grandfather was very famous for raising money for institutions like Barnard College, Philips Exeter Academy, and Amherst College. And he used to study the people — they were these difficult men with lots of money. He would find out their hobbies or what they enjoy talking about ... and how not to antagonize them.

Vault: Do you do that with people?

Plimpton: I think you have to prepare a little bit before when seeing somebody who is going to be difficult, either with a story you've heard the day before or something else which shows that you're making an attempt to bridge the gap between the two of you.

Vault: When you meet people, do you often think "I can talk to this person for an article"?

Plimpton: If it's about writing, then I do make a note, sure. I met someone the other day in a restaurant who evinced a great interest in helping out the *Paris Review* financially. So obviously I jotted down his name and we had lunch the next day.

Vault: Do you find people try to schmooze you? People who you might not know that will try to get in touch with you?

Plimpton: Oh, yeah. Last night I was having dinner at a restaurant and someone just

Plimpton interview, cont'd...

came to the table. He was a reporter for *The Washington Post.* He said I wrote an article that really affected him about seven years ago. I told him, 'Do sit down.' He sat down with his date.

Vault: And he stayed with you the rest of the evening?

Plimpton: Yes.

Vault: At the *Paris Review,* do you find yourself giving them a lot of advice on how to make connections, or career advice? Do young employees come to you for that?

Plimpton: Well, every once in a while ... People here at the magazine are all 22, 23, 24, so they are in a position of asking for it. They all are at the level of wanting to know what to do next. It's sort of a jumping-off base here ... In publishing I think you have to have a love of books, a certain knowledge of how to write, a certain knowledge of marketing. It's one of the industries I think that you learn as you go along, but the first step, the open door, is very hard, because there are so few jobs.

I think at the magazine you learn how to read manuscripts, you learn the travails of magazines, you learn something about writing. You learn about the functions of a writers' commune. It's like any milieu – you learn something about the milieu itself, which is important if you want to be in publishing, because you get to know editors at publishing houses, you get to know magazine editors.

Vault: As far as communicating with people, knowing people, getting in touch with people, and bringing people together, who is the best you ever met?

Plimpton: I suppose Mrs. Onassis.

Vault: Why do you think she was so good at it?

Plimpton: All you've got to do is pick up the phone and say, 'I'm Mrs. Onassis.'

Vault: *(laugh)* How do you think others who are not Jacqueline Onassis can do it? Just pick up the phone anyway?

Plimpton: Yeah. Well, I remember President Bush saying this, and indeed Jackie saying, that the wonderful thing about their position was they could get anybody in the world on the phone.

I'm in a rather nice position too, because I'm known through television and through sports and through having written popular books, and so yeah, I pick up the phone and get to somebody.

Vault: Now, you can say 'I was in *Good Will Hunting* and people would know the movie ... Matt Damon and Ben Affleck are sort of my idea of young people who broke through.

Plimpton: Well, they're certainly good at what they do, but also ... because of Matt Damon's work on *The Rainmaker,* they met Gus Van Zant, and because of that they were able to push the thing through. That's all part of it. Especially in Hollywood. If you don't know anybody in Hollywood, you just can't get anywhere.

Vault: Guess it's a matter of getting to know that first person.

Plimpton: It's about getting to know that first person. Right.

Sensitivity to others

Let's stop for a minute and think about what the preceding sections – doing research, taking an interest and paying attention, listening, finding similarities – were essentially about. They're about concerning yourself with the other person. Advanced schmoozing involves picking up clues from others.

That's why the importance of similarity extends to body language. Salespeople are taught to mirror the movements of their clients in both their own body language and their overall tone – you can take these lessons into your own schmoozing. If another person's body language is very open, then respond accordingly. If they lean a bit forward, so do you. If the other person is deliberate and makes few gestures, gesticulating wildly is not a good idea.

When we think about the importance of concentrating on the person we are speaking with, we understand all that stereotypical lawyerly rhetoric in the courtroom. J. Owen Todd, the Boston trial lawyer, explains that "the principal element involved in trial practice is communicating with people." Toward this end, lawyers are "communicating in the sense of revisiting the scene, taking them back," Todd explains. This is why, he says, lawyers say things like, "You will be there. This is what you'll see.'"

Our fundraiser Juliet Gumbs tells an anecdote that perfectly captures the importance of understanding how and why the people we meet work the way they do. Gumbs left a position with an academic institution to join Poets and Writers, a group that raises money for artists. She says that when she told people of her move, many were virtually aghast. "They said, 'Why would anyone ever give to an organization like that? No one ever asked these people to be artists. They can do other things. They don't compare to the child in the Third World who is going hungry.'" Gumbs knew otherwise. "They didn't understand that it isn't about the recipient," she says. "It's about what the giver gets."

Do favors

Schmoozing is not about exploiting or taking from people. In fact, the best schmoozers are as generous as possible. Mark Hernandez, a principal at Blackburg, an online derivatives trading company, explains how he has schmoozed Latin American clients. "You invest a lot by teaching them [about finance], so they owe you." Of course, it's not just about doing favors professionally. Hernandez takes his clients out on the town when he travels in South America, so they enjoy his visits. "You show them a good time," he says.

Doing a minor favor for someone inevitably triggers a reciprocal response. This apparently works even for unexpected favors. If you help someone with their bags or get them a drink – and if they accept it – you trigger in them a sense of obligation. In the early 1970s, Denis Regan of Cornell University performed an experiment in which two people – one of whom was actually posing as a subject – rated paintings, ostensibly as part of a study on art appreciation. The two people were given a break during their rating session.

In some cases, the person posing as a subject left the room and returned with two Cokes, one for the real subject. The poser explained that he had asked the person running the experiment if he could get a drink, and when told he could, decided to buy one for the other person, too. In other cases, the person posing as a subject simply left and came back empty-handed. After the session was over, the person posing as a subject asked the real subject to buy raffle tickets. Those subjects who received Cokes purchased twice as many tickets as those who had not.

Our Home is Your Home

Running a bed and breakfast (or "B&B") isn't just a job, it's a never-ending schmoozathon. B&B customers aren't just clients, but temporary guests who stay in their hosts' homes. What's it like to be schmoozing 24 hours a day, 7 days a week? We asked Lois and Bud Ellison, who run a B&B called Limestone Manor, in Florence, Alabama. Their inn — built by a mayor of Florence in the late 19th century — has two guest rooms (one fits two guests and one fits four). The Ellisons say they enjoy the small size and intimacy of their inn, which allows them to pay personal attention to each guest.

House special: heart-shaped French toast

Originally from California, the Ellisons say everyone in Florence has been welcoming, in part "because we made sure to get involved in community activities right away." Even before they started their business, in other words, they started schmoozing.

To open their business, Lois and Bud had to get approval through the city, which is home to the University of North Alabama and located on the Tennessee River. "We joined the Chamber of Commerce and the North Alabama Mountain Lakes Associates, which promotes tourism," says Lois Ellison. "We also invited people from the university to visit. We had a luncheon for them and established a relationship. Now we often get referrals from the university, when there are guests they can't put up themselves." The Ellisons do other favors for the university – not charging for people meeting for breakfast at the B&B, for example, when prospective faculty members stay. Bud Ellison is in charge of the couple's community outreach effort. He consistently talks to people in the community and performs small charity actions, like donating gift certificates for Jaycee raffles.

WHAT IT TAKES

"It has occurred to me that there are two very important attributes necessary to succeed in the B&B business: flexibility and a sense of humor," Lois Ellison says. "Each guest is unique and you must be able to adjust to their needs. Sometimes you have to change direction very quickly so you need to remain alert to unspoken signals and be ready to gracefully adapt. You have to be prepared to address all sorts of situations with charm and dignity. Not just cooking and cleaning, but also plumbing, first aid, electrical problems, insects, etc. It's not always easy to smile and reassure your guests that everything is OK when they tell you that the toilet is overflowing onto the brand-new flooring! You also need that sense of humor so you can laugh after the problems are resolved and also, most important, to laugh at yourself when needed."

How much do the Ellisons interact with their guests? "You need to see how much they want from you," says Lois Ellison. "If they are inclined to talk, we love to chat. We had some people stay for a week, and we became very friendly and had dinner together a few times. We also had guests for a four-night stay that included Christmas, so we all spent Christmas together." Ellison says she makes personalized cards and adds "special little touches," such as making heart-shaped French toast for couples celebrating their anniversaries. And every visitor "has a plate of some kind of goodie in their room when they arrive, brownies or muffins."

Ellison credits the Internet — Limestone Manor's web site went up soon after the inn opened — with helping her husband and her start their business. "There is a lot of turnover in this business and the books on bed and breakfasts that you find in the store have a two-year lag time," she explains.

But as one might expect of an old-fashioned hospitality business like a bed and breakfast, an old-fashioned, simple thank you is still the most effective

Our Home is Your Home, cont'd...

marketing tool. The Ellisons have postcards made of the Limestone Manor, which they mail with personalized notes out to guests the day they leave. One guest, after receiving his postcard, called to say that he had traveled on business for years and never gotten a thank-you note from any hotel or inn. Guess who's been back to visit with the Ellisons?

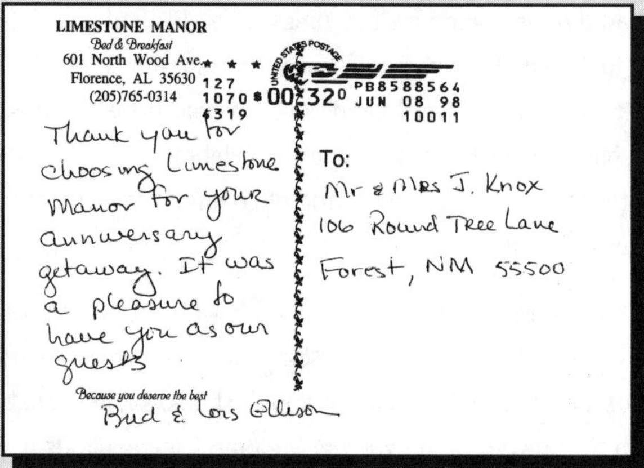

How the Ellisons follow up with guests

Although giving favors may provoke a reciprocal response, for a schmoozer it's about generosity, not expecting to get something in return. Craig Enenstein uses what he calls "the Godfather principle." "Remember that scene in the beginning when the guy comes to ask the Don to kill the guys who beat up his daughter?" Enenstein says. "Don Corleone says, 'I may call on you for a small favor, maybe never.' That's how I feel."

"I feel that I should do as much as possible for people I care about, people I respect, people I think might be worth doing something for. I expect nothing back," he says. "My philosophy is that I do things for people far above and beyond what they expect. But I do hope — though I never demand — that one day if I need something I can call on them. There have been some disappointments but 90 percent of the time they help me."

TOUCH?

When schmoozing people previously unknown to you, you must be careful not to give the wrong impression. You're schmoozing to connect on a social level, not a romantic one (at least at first). To make your schmoozee feel more comfortable, try not to stare at them. While standards vary between societies, in America it's generally acceptable to look at someone for about seven seconds, then look away for seven seconds or so. Refrain from looking anywhere but your schmoozee's face. Avoid making comments about clothing or personal features that may be misinterpreted.

OK: What a handsome purse. Did you buy it in Italy?

Iffy: I like that suit – it fits you very well.

No way: That tight blouse flatters your large breasts.

People have different reactions to touch; some people are "touchers" who like to touch and be touched as they talk, while others don't normally enjoy casual physical contact. Worse, some people may misinterpret a touch, even on neutral areas of the body such as the hand or arm. You should simply follow your schmoozee's lead. If you are ever uncomfortable, politely disengage yourself.

Jim, our school board head from Connecticut, explains his guidelines: "It depends on the situation. There are times, when I try to reach out and touch somebody on the arm to reinforce the meeting. If it's a woman, I'm very careful, it's a handshake and no other body contact, other than I might touch an elbow."

The power of indirect thinking

When it comes to getting your friends and acquaintances to help you, good schmoozers know that people are most likely and willing to do something if they think it's their idea. That's why you should avoid asking for something outright. Most people, if they are so inclined, will genuinely want to help you, but their definitions of help may not dovetail exactly with yours.

Glenda Wilson, a UNICEF fundraiser, says that "the best way to schmooze is to be subtle. You cannot hit people over the head with what you want. For example, if you know someone has a condo in Rio that you want to use, a direct approach could put people on the spot and make them less likely to help. Don't ask them if you can use it, but mention that you are traveling to Rio and need suggestions for a good hotel."

Tamarah Totah, a former headhunter for an executive search firm in New York, stresses one major thing when schmoozing for a job: "Don't put them on the spot." Totah follows her own advice. She explains that when she contacted people she believed would be well-suited for a position – especially if she had to leave a message on an answering machine – she approached indirectly with lines like "I don't know if you'd be interested, but maybe somebody you know might be."

Bridgett Bailee, our former Mary Kay Cosmetics director in San Antonio, Texas, says salespeople are cautioned not to beat others over the head with mentions of the wondrous products of their employer. "It's like a cat and mouse game. It's like having a piece of cheese on a string. You mention Mary Kay, then you talk about something else, you draw back the string. You do that again and again."

CONJUNCTION JUNCTION, WHAT'S YOUR FUNCTION?

Pay attention to verbal cues. Harvard psychologist Ellen Langer, in her oft-cited "copy machine studies," found that when one of her agents approached someone at a photocopier and asked, "May I use the copy machine?" they were allowed to skip ahead about 60 percent of the time. But those who asked, "May I use the copy machine, because I'm in a rush?" received access nearly 95 percent of the time. Do you think that citing a convincing reason for their hurry made the difference? Well, when Langer had the interrupter ask "May I use the copy machine, because I need to make some copies?" the results were similar. Again, nearly 95 percent of the subjects stepped aside. The key was not the reason, but the use of the word "because." People hearing the word "because" in connection with a minor favor automatically performed the favor.

This doesn't mean that "because" is your magic ticket. When Langer sent interrupters with armfuls of copies, people stopped and judged the reason behind the request.. In this case, saying "because I have to make some copies" had no effect. Only when a plausible reason was given would others consider stepping aside.

Some other handy conjunctions:

When making a correction, altering a request, or giving constructive criticism, replace "but" with "and." Let's say you're schmoozing for a job, and someone mentions a friend in a field completely unrelated to what you want to do. It would be wrong and ungrateful to say:

"Thank you so much for your help, but do you know anyone in publishing?"

But try saying:

"Thank you so much for your help, and do you know anyone in publishing?"

The thanks flows directly into your next request and softens the fact that you're asking for something new.

But you can't get anything without asking, right? Don't be ridiculous. Our schmoozy apartment finder and political consultant, Marla, says, "Of course I know what people are doing when they ask for something indirectly. But it offends me to be asked outright for something, especially by someone I don't know that well." She continues, "If someone talked about how they wanted to go to a concert but couldn't get tickets, and I knew someone who could help out, then I would. But for example, I was in a friend's office, and the receptionist, who knew I could get tickets, started bugging me about getting them, and there is no way I would help out someone like that."

GETTING PEOPLE TO JUST SAY NO

Although much has been said and written about the attempts in conversation to "get to yes," depending on how you size up your schmoozee, "no" may be the answer you're looking for. Bridgett Bailee, a former director for Mary Kay cosmetics in San Antonio, Texas, says that during training of salespeople: "We are told that it's easier to say 'no' than 'yes.'" What does this mean practically? "You should phrase a question so that the answer you want is "no." Say something like "Is there any reason I can't call you about this?" Mary Kay estimates that 70 percent of the time, you'll get the answer you want."

Not only can asking directly and specifically turn people off, but it can also limit what you might get. Beth Calabro, the former in-house producer at Miramax Films, explains, "So many people call up agents and they say, 'Oh send me a script about this and this.' They're so specific, they don't get good material. I try to be very broad. I find that's the best way to do it."

Remember, you're schmoozing. Don't set limits, and be patient. Even if people know that they are in a position to help you, they won't necessarily volunteer that information right away. Give them time.

You're the greatest!

Even if you apparently don't have anything in common with your intended schmoozee right off the bat, there is one way to get on their good side right away – flattery. People feel good when they are complimented and transfer those good feelings to the person. Likewise, when someone is seen insulting or degrading someone, others transfer the negative feelings he is expressing to the person himself. Yes, we do still shoot the messenger. But you can be the messenger who's invited to stay for dinner (see inset on next page).

Flattery shows that you've noticed something positive about the object of your schmoozing. Let's face it – people want to think the best of themselves. Don't lie for the sake of flattery, though. A patently untrue compliment is easy to see through, often backfires badly, and only hurts your schmoozing karma.

But if you genuinely feel that someone did a wonderful job on her latest project, or that the man in the parking lot has a terrific vintage Austin Healey car, go ahead and say so. Everyone likes a genuine compliment. If you feel that it would be "sucking up" or insincere, try just a little bit of flattery. Tell your favorite street food vendor that his hot dogs are always hot, sanitary and delicious. Pat a co-worker on the back for getting an important report done in time.

"I often compliment women on a truly sharp outfit," says Bridgett Bailee, the former Mary Kay director. "I tell them that I have to look good everywhere I go when I travel for my job. I'll ask them for the address of where they bought the suit. I can also usually spot Estee Lauder or Clinique makeup. I will tell them I like it and ask, 'What color is it? Mary Kay is always looking for good new colors.' All I want is a conversation and ultimately to get their number or e-mail address."

SHOOTING THE MESSENGER

It's called spontaneous trait transference. It's the reason that weathermen are often threatened when it rains too much, and why airline employees bear the brunt of travelers' anger when flights are delayed. And it's why, in ancient Greece, messengers who ran great distances to deliver bad news were, um, dispatched.

When we give good or bad news, or when we speak of the good or bad traits of others, our audiences assign the same traits to us. Research at Ohio State and Purdue University published in 1998 bears this out. The researchers found that traits such as faithfulness, dependability, dishonesty, even clumsiness, were associated with people who assigned those characteristics to others. About 250 student subjects were tested in a variety of ways. In some cases, they were shown pictures of a person with a printed statement such as: "I saw her run down the court and dunk the ball." In another part of the study, subjects watched videotapes of actors answering questions about themselves and someone they knew.

Across the board, the researchers found, when the text underneath the pictures was taken away, or the actors were shown without the dialogue, subjects continued to associate the described traits with the pictures. In one oft-cited example, a speaker describing a person as an animal-hater who was seen kicking a puppy was later described as cruel by the subjects.

The experiment essentially backs up all those sayings about criticism we learned as children. If you can't say something nice, don't say it at all. I'm rubber and you're glue – it's all true.

An especially refined and effective form of flattery, our schmoozing pros tell us, is asking for advice. Everyone wants to feel like they're an authority about something. "If you ask someone to do something for you, they probably won't," advises Glenda Wilson. "But if you ask them to tell you about something or ask them to help you, they are much more likely to do what you want."

Asking for advice can also be a way of paying a third person a compliment. For example, you might call someone and say, "Hi, Eloise. Adam tells me that you're a terrific actress whom he admires very much. I'd love to hear about how you got into the business." Not only does this position you as someone Eloise can help, Eloise also has the gratifying experience of hearing that Adam thinks she's terrific. Her positive feelings will be transferred to Adam — and to you.

Finish with a flourish

All of your skillful schmoozing will be worthless if you don't finish your conversations gracefully. Whether we realize it or not, there are conventions that need to be followed when we break off a conversation. "There are egos involved," notes Kathryn Dindia. "No one wants to feel like they're boring." What this means is that, when you end a conversation, supply some kind of excuse. At a party, that might be "Excuse me, I have to get a drink," or "Oh, I promised I'd speak to Deborah over there. Pardon me." Otherwise, your excuse might be as simple as "I'm sorry, I'm running late," or "I have to meet someone."

Another concern when a conversation ends is that the relationship itself might be ending. (This is clearly not as much of an issue with long-term relationships, where people feel comfortable saying "Gotta go.") That's why, says Dindia, we commonly end conversations with "See you later," or "I'll call you." Look at two ways to end a conversation that essentially convey the same information:

> "I have to go. Good-bye."
>
> "I've got to run along, but I'll talk to you later, OK?"

The first conversation ending sounds harsh and cold, while the second is friendly and invites further contact — the perfect note for the good schmoozer to hit.

Schmoozer, be not discouraged

Now that you know the building blocks of schmoozing, you're set to begin your schmoozing career. Just remember that not every schmoozing attempt works. Some people may be preoccupied or angry for some reason that has nothing to do with you. Smile, wish them a nice day, and move on. You'll find with time that your successes far outweigh any missteps. Remember that most of your schmoozing conversations will not benefit you or affect the course of your life in any way — except to make it richer and more enjoyable. Consultant Craig Enenstein sums up: "For me the whole thing is about establishing a meaningful, broad group of contacts which will ultimately help you expand your knowledge, your opportunities and enjoyment. Anytime I have a question, need a favor, or just want to have dinner with someone, there's always someone I can call."

Vault Profile: Craig Enenstein

Craig Enenstein is a self-described "planner" who's always mapped out his future – and yet at the same time has accounted for an element of flexibility. At age 15, young Craig decided that he wanted to pursue a life building a huge global business.

Enenstein has kept his eyes on his prize – and he's made sure that others are watching too. Enenstein diligently keeps former colleagues and classmates informed about his career trajectory. "I do it in conversations, and I send out a lot of holiday cards every year," he says. "Normally, it's around 400 people, but we had 700 this year. We pre-print around six lines on each card, with an update on us, what I'm doing, what my wife is doing, and what goals we hope to achieve. It takes us a few days to figure out how to write an appropriate message in a few lines."

Craig wants to buy your company

After graduating from UC Berkeley, Enenstein accepted a position with a major Japanese trading company and later started his own firm in Tokyo. He came back to the States to get an MBA from the Wharton School of Finance and an MA in international studies at the University of Pennsylvania (a dual degree he completed in 24 months straight). During school, Enenstein, who was known for giving career advice to his classmates, solidified his own career goals, deciding eventually to build his own private equity firm (a company that invests money by buying other companies). Before taking his current position with Los Angeles-based Knowledge Universe, he was a management consultant for Bain & Company and LEK/Alcar.

Enenstein profile, cont'd...

Today, Enenstein is a member of the M&A team at Knowledge Universe, an integrated global education company backed by well-known finance specialist Michael Milken, his brother Lowell Milken, and Oracle CEO Larry Ellison, currently building itself by gobbling up other education companies.

Enenstein's current position is partly a product of his devotion to keeping in touch. While most of us are thrilled when we find we have one contact at a company that can help us get a foot in the door, Enenstein had several forces actually pulling him into the firm. "I had two acquaintances from business school who worked here, and one from a previous job, so they called me," he says. "While I had to interview with the entire firm, the toughest part about getting into this industry is even knowing that an opportunity exists. I know people who would kill to have that opportunity."

KEY CONCEPTS

- Find a reason to socialize.
- Enjoy yourself.
- Don't view setbacks as permanent.
- Pay attention to others and concentrate.
- Research those you will meet.
- Listen actively.
- Find similarities.
- Do favors.
- Ask for what you want indirectly.
- Flattery will get you somewhere.

America's Top Schmoozers

1. **Oprah Winfrey:** When Oprah talks, people listen. But what really makes her an all-star, is that when people talk, Oprah listens. With a No. 1 talk show — 16 years running! — and now a hit magazine and a stake in Oxygen Media, Oprah truly is the queen of all media. And she got there by being the queen of schmooze.

2. **Arnold Schwarzenegger:** From an unpronounceable to a household name, Arnold has assiduously worked his way to stardom. Along the way, he married into that most schmoozy of families, the Kennedys, and managed to snag a post as the nation's fitness guru in the first Bush administration. We could cap this off by emulating one of those lame-ass puns that Arnie uses when he finishes off a bad guy, but we'd raaather not.

3. **Sean "P Diddy" Combs:** Despite his changing styles and nicknames, one thing remains constant about this chameleon: his schmooze appeal. The Grammy-winning rapper, fashion designer, restaurant owner, and Hamptons socialite emerged from his 2001 trial on weapons and bribery charges (stemming from a shooting in a NYC nightclub) virtually unscathed — he was acquitted but soon afterward lost his girlfriend Jennifer Lopez. Reports say Combs may be trying to woo back JLo with his hit song, "I Need a Girl," (featuring the lyricis: "I need a girl to make my wife..."). Will this schmoozemeister win her back into his life once again?

4. **Herb Allen:** Allen and his investment banking company (called Allen & Company) are host to the nation's biggest schmoozefest, an annual retreat in Sun Valley, Idaho, where Allen schmoozes with the biggest names in high tech and entertainment. To be invited is to be a player.

5. **George Plimpton:** Plimpton's mop of white hair can be spotted everywhere. Watch the documentary *When We Were Kings* about the famous Muhammad Ali/George Foreman fight – and there Plimpton is, watching

Foreman take a tumble. Ruffle through the pages of *The New Yorker*, there he is again, penning a piece about one of his many adventures. Flip the channel to get away from the highbrow, ready to watch the "Married With Children" 100th episode, there he is again. Plimpton recently authored *Truman Capote, In Which Various Friends, Enemies, Acquaintances, and Detractors Recall His Turbulent Career.* No schmoozing barriers for this literary lion! (see interview, p. 72)

6. **Regis Philbin:** Philbin's success is rooted in the fundamental principles of the schmoozer. He is relentlessly upbeat, despite more than his fair share of obstacles in life. He keeps in touch with as many people as he can and he's always trying to do favors for others without expecting favors in return. This is also the man who catapulted "Is that your final answer?" into everyday conversation; and who spawned a clothing line with his signature monochromatic shirt and satin tie combo. And Philbin proved whom America was really tuning in to see when the ratings for *Live!* actually peaked rather than dipped upon Kathie Lee Gifford's departure.

7. **Larry King:** Yes, we know about his gazillion wives. Half gossip-columnist (read his bits in *USA Today*) and half talk show host, Larry practices the art of flattery none too subtly. But then again, it doesn't matter. Politicos and celebs gladly proffer their cheeks for a little of King's puckering. King proves that if you say good things about people and give them the opportunity to speak their mind, they'll think well of you.

8. **Liz Smith:** A national institution, Liz Smith is America's "Grand Dame of Dish." Unlike most people in the gossip trade, Smith doesn't have many enemies. In fact, she's wooed and courted by movie stars, politicians, socialites, and anyone else who has the red carpet rolled out for them on a regular basis — anything to get a mere mention in her daily column, which is syndicated in more than 70 newspapers nationwide. With her autobiography, *Natural Blonde*, released in the fall of 2000, Smith has created a whole new venue in which to hobnob: book signings, book readings, and book parties.

9. **Willie Brown:** One of the country's most popular mayors, Brown is notoriously high-flying and quick-witted. (Upon being offered either the Lincoln or the Queen's Bedroom in the White House, he said: "Being from San Francisco, I'm cognizant of the queens' vote, but I think I'll go with the man who freed me.") As famous as his wit is his prodigious memory (a powerful schmoozing tool), which allows him to store reams of regulations and stats on subjects like traffic accidents or land use policy. Finally, this former shoeshine boy who worked his way through law school as a janitor plays the games of favor-granting and fundraising well, skills that kept him at the head of the state legislature for an unprecedented 14 years. (see profile, p. 283)

10. **Jeff Bezos:** This man may have brought the art of schmoozing to a whole new level. He has somehow convinced the world, not to mention *Time* magazine (which named him 1999's Person of the Year), that his in-the-red company is a leader in the e-commerce industry. Revolutionary? Maybe. Profitable? Well, not until the fourth quarter of 2001! When he was named Person of the Year, his only request was that the news be broken on *Live! With Regis and Kathie Lee.* It takes a schmoozer to know one.

CHAPTER 5

WHO DO YOU KNOW?

You're connected already

"Start with what you know," conventional fortune cookie wisdom tells us. The schmoozing fortune cookie reads: "Start with *who* you know." This simple tenet of schmoozing assumes that there are people who you do know and with whom you can schmooze. And you do. Everybody knows somebody. In fact, you probably know more people than you think.

You might think glumly upon reading this last sentence. "Perhaps everyone else knows somebody, but I'm just a recent college graduate and I have no connections whatsoever." Or perhaps you're worried that you've been out of the workforce for some time. Or that your only true friends are your goldfish Petra and Flynn — and they aren't great conversationalists.

Fear not! This chapter will show you how to tap into your immediate schmoozing circle of friends and family. The people you know right now serve two immediate schmoozing purposes. First, they are the perfect audience for your initial schmoozing experiments. Second, they're usually readily accessible. Where do you hear about that great new account executive slot that's just opened up? From schmoozing the people in your circle of friends, family and acquaintances. Where do you hear about that fabulous restaurant that's just opened or get a tip on that impossibly cheap studio sublet? The people you know.

Whether or not you're looking for a job, having a wide circle of friends and acquaintances immeasurably enriches your life. Keep this in mind as you read. Even if you're sure a person can't do anything for your career or love life, do whatever you can for them. It feels good to acknowledge and help someone, and they'll remember your kindness in the future. And you never know when the seemingly least significant member of your network will suddenly take on great importance. Let's take a look at who you know.

The family

Your parents and immediate family are your biggest boosters. Enlist them as allies in your schmoozing army. The same zeal that led your parents to call 20 toy stores in search of that perfect Hot Wheels for your birthday can be harnessed to beat the bushes for whatever else your little heart desires, whether that's a hot job lead or a good price on a beachside condo.

One of the reasons we don't ask our family members for help is that we feel so familiar with Mom, Dad, Bro and Sis that we can't imagine they have resources we're unaware of, so we don't bother asking them for help. Or, conversely, we are afraid of the taint of nepotism and want to feel we're past the point of asking Mommy and Daddy for a leg up. Or we might be reluctant to fill in our parents on our job aspirations, because we don't want them to nag us incessantly. Or perhaps we've always been considered the "artistic one," and we're hesitant to tell sis that we've decided to become an accountant.

Put these outdated issues aside. Not taking advantage of these closest of contacts puts you at a disadvantage. The research of psychologist George Dudley indicates that real estate agents who don't call on family members sell, on the average, $6,000 less per month than those who do.

Your pals

As impressive as an average of $6,000 a month in sales for a real estate agent might be, Dudley's research shows that ignoring friends can be even more of a disadvantage than ignoring family. Agents who don't call on friends bring in about $20,500 less a month, according to his research. Automobile salespeople earn 15.5 percent less if they don't tap into their friends.

You generally can tell your close friends anything and are comfortable leaning on them for support. If you need a favor, you can be reasonably direct (though usually not as forthcoming as you'd be with your family). You can tell your dad to pick you up at the airport – you'd have to cajole a friend. In any case, always remember that schmoozing is a matter of caring about and enjoying the company of others. Don't lean on your friends too strongly for job leads or other favors – simply let them know what you need, and keep the channels of schmoozing and communication open.

But as with close family members, don't make the erroneous assumption that you know absolutely everything about your best pal from kindergarten. Your close friends may have friends and interests that can expand the potential pool of people to meet and schmooze. And remember that your friends may make the same mistake – assuming that you're already familiar with their stint at Walt Disney or their buddy who sells yachts.

Vault Interview: A.J. Benza, TV Personality

"When you have a position in a New York City paper, especially as a columnist, and when you wield the kind of power that only a New York City columnist can yield, you have a lot of people who need you for help," says former New York Daily News *gossip columnist A.J. Benza. "A lot of people come at you, and a lot of those favors get repaid."*

Jack, can I call you back?

Benza, 35, has since left the world of gossip for the world of TV and movies – but he still keeps in touch with friends "Jack" and "Warren" (that's Nicholson and Beatty). Since moving to Hollywood, Benza has been busy. He published an autobiography, is hosting Mysteries and Scandals, *a show on E! Entertainment, had a role in* Ransom *with Mel Gibson and Renee Russo, has made another independent movie with Steven Segal, and is developing a late-night talk show. Still, he says that he flies back to New York to hang out with his old friends. "The guys I run with are the same guys I've run with for the last 15 years. Their names are like Rocko, Vinny Boy and Chico and Frankie. They keep me grounded ... You don't make better friends than you do when you're 10, 15 years old."*

Vault.com interviewed Benza about his rise from a sportswriter with Newsday *to a player in the entertainment world. Here are some excerpts.*

Vault: When you were talking about how people needed you in your *Daily News* days what did you mean by that?

Benza: Especially when you're dealing with Hollywood types and movie types and publishing types and music types, people need good publicity, people need certain stories out there.

Vault: So celebrities would actually contact you?

Benza: Some celebrities would. Absolutely. There were some celebrities that would contact me when there was a problem in their lives. When they anticipated a scandal, so to speak. There were several big-time celebrities who needed to speak with me and said, "Maybe we can fix this," and "'Maybe we can frame it in a certain way." Now, I'd be lying if I said I never got anything back in return for those things that I did.

Vault: What kinds of favors would they do?

Benza: Well, you know, sometimes some of the biggest celebrities in the world would give you a story on someone else as long as you balanced their little scandal. And if I was a big fan of the celebrity, in most cases I would silence the scandal. My goal was to come out of the gossip field with a lot of stars and celebrities and powerful people on my side. It's very easy to alienate those people. If you really want to go at the core of scandals that exist in this town, you can alienate yourself from everyone powerful. That was never my objective.

Vault: How did you get up to this position of power?

Benza: It was totally by surprise. I was married and then I got divorced. Once I got divorced I started going out on the town a lot — I was always drawn to Manhattan. I was a part-time sportswriter at *Newsday,* and then I started helping out on the gossip page at New York *Daily News.* And once I was on the gossip columns, or helping out on the gossip columns, I was given all these invitations to parties and openings and galas, you name it, and it didn't take long before people started giving you winks, throwing you a couple of beers. You'd mention their restaurant in an item, mention their club, mention their client, and, you know, all of a sudden the invitations pour in, and the favors pour in, and you become ... a little powerful.

Vault: How long did it take from...

Benza: From where I was a regular guy? In 1992, I couldn't get past a velvet rope in any part of the city. I couldn't get into a private party or a nightclub. I'd say about a

Benza interview, cont'd...

year and a half. I was in, in like Flynn. I was at the *Daily News*, I was a gossip columnist. There wasn't a door that wasn't opened for me, there wasn't a meal that wasn't sent over, there wasn't a drink that wasn't bought ... whatever I wanted, if I really let it be known that I wanted it, I got it.

Vault: As you developed into that power, I know that you said you got calls from celebrities, but did you also ever get calls from assistants?

Benza: Often, what really stinks is a celebrity pays a publicist or a manager or a press agent to keep his life in order, to keep things out of the press. What ends up happening all the time, these stars don't realize that these same people they pay to protect them, all they have to do is be disgruntled a little bit and they're dropping bombs on the same people that pay them. At the beginning it was kind of fun, and then you felt a little scandalous getting the news.

Vault: Would they approach you first, or would you have to get them to trust you?

Benza: You have to develop a trust with people. Once you hang around publicists and you really get to know them, they get to schmooze you, you get to schmooze them, there's a nice trust that develops. Don't forget, every publicist has several different clients that they have an interest in. One publicist may handle Sylvester Stallone, and they might also handle a restaurant or nightclub, or a fashion magazine. If they needed a plug for their fashion magazine's Christmas party, or if they needed a plug for the new underwear line at Structure, in turn, you're gonna say, "Well look, I need something juicy from you."

Vault: How do you make sure that the star doesn't know who's giving you the stories?

Benza: You never let anybody know that publicist really well. If a certain publicist is at a function with Sylvester Stallone, I'm not going to run up and hug that person alone. I'm not going to act like we're the best of buddies, I'm not going to act like that person's dropped a dime on him or someone close to him. So once that publicist sees that you can be trusted ... this applies also to agents and managers ... you name it. Once those people see that you can be trusted, they sweat the night out and they say 'Wow, well, that worked out fine, I got my thing in the paper, and A.J. got his story. Hey, good.

Vault: So it's tit for tat?

Benza: That's all it is. I wish I could tell you that a lot of it is really hard, in-the-trenches reporting, but bullshit. You sit at your phone, and you wait for a secret to come across your desk.

Vault: How will you know when to ask for a little more from friends like Jack Nicholson and Warren Beatty?

Benza: I've always had a good sense of timing, and I've always felt that a good way to judge when to push it is when you get more calls from those people than you're making. And right now, I'm not. And there might be a day when they invite me to their house a little more often than they do now, and when those days come , and when you make a few of those guys laugh at a party over and over again, maybe it's time to say, 'Hey, you know what? I want you to check this out.'

Vault: Do you call them every once in a while?

Benza: Yeah, of course. Not frequently, but I let them know I'm around. I let Warren know *I love Bulworth*, I let Jack know he should win the Oscar. Yeah, I make those calls, and maybe seven times out of 10 you get the assistant, but those three times that Jack or Warren or (producer) Bob Evans call back, you feel like a million bucks.

Not gone, not forgotten

Your sophomore-year college roommate, that guy with whom you used to play racquetball, that Henry James fan in your book club who moved to Seattle – these are all people you can get back in touch with to enlarge your sphere of schmoozing. Even if you haven't spoken to some of these old friends and acquaintances for years, don't be afraid to get back in touch with them.

Lara Rosenthal, a freelance writer in New York who spent time in Asia and also worked for the Dow Jones China bureau, says, "Some people I don't see for years. Some people, particularly people in China I know and like but don't see very often, I'll e-mail them once a year. If I think about them, I'll call them. I don't feel like I need to check in with anyone. When I was in Hong Kong, I called someone I hadn't seen in three or four years and it was fine."

It's important to conquer your initial resistance. Perhaps you already have the phone number and e-mail and home address of your old friends, and they have yours. But it's been a while since you've heard from them. Or perhaps you've completely lost touch; the only contact point now is that tattered old address book you think is somewhere under your bed. "Forget it," you may say. "They know where to find me." Or: "Forget it. They probably don't even remember me." There are a few factors at work here – fear that you've been forgotten (and are therefore forgettable), annoyance (that your erstwhile pal hasn't taken the trouble to get in touch), and inertia (the same reluctance to stretch yourself that prevents your old friends from getting in touch with you).

Forget all that. Be the one who makes something happen and call. Look at it this way: in the worst case scenario, in the rare instance that they've forgotten you, they'll probably be apologetic and friendly. On the other hand, they may very well be thrilled to hear from you. Remember that part of schmoozing is creating an atmosphere of enjoyment and relaxation – and your old friends are already positively inclined toward you.

"I recently found a news item that an alum had donated $40 million to a school and I forwarded it on to all my Kellogg people," says one California-based consultant. "I hadn't spoken to some of them in 18 months. One sent back an e-mail that said 'Dan, that's fascinating, please give me a call.'"

Even if you haven't been as conscientious as Dan, feel free through to go through your old alumni directory or discarded Rolodex – it's a surefire way to expand your schmoozing universe. It's flattering to be re-contacted out of the blue. And once you get back in touch, stay in touch. Ex-Girl Scouts may remember the old saying: "Make new friends, but keep the old. One is silver and the other gold." The saying simply means that shared memories and history make any connection stronger, and time doesn't have the power to weaken friendship as much as we think it does.

Kith and kin

We've passed the age of the close-knit extended family. While some people still keep in close touch with all their aunts and uncles and cousins and second cousins, shrinking family size and the increased mobility of modern life means that your family may not be occupying much space on your speed dial. But don't ignore the power of blood ties. Even if you think you've got nothing in common with your cousin Heidi, or you haven't spoken to great-uncle Charles in 15 years, or there's some sort of vague decade-long family feud about a piece of heirloom china going on, it's still appropriate to get back in touch.

You already have something in common (family ties) that gives you something to talk about. And you can make societal dispersion work to your advantage as well. For example, if you're planning a move to another city, or simply need a good restaurant recommendation, chances are you may already have a relative there. Take advantages of the times you see your relatives – family reunions, weddings, Thanksgiving dinners. Treat your relatives like valued friends, not like background scenery. It will enrich both your life and your schmoozing.

Brian Fox tells of a time when schmoozing at a family occasion served him well. He was reluctant to attend the traditional family Thanksgiving dinner, filled as it normally was with cranky aunts and uncles and barely remembered cousins. But Brian persevered and was soon seated next to his cousin Wendy, whom he hadn't seen in a decade. Brian could tell from Wendy's blank gaze that she barely remembered him. Yet Brian persevered, and soon the two were happily chatting about Wendy's ill-fated childhood pet hamster. When the subject turned to jobs, Brian confessed that he was searching for a position in advertising. It turned out that Wendy now worked for a job placement agency and helped her cousin find a job. If Brian had managed to weasel out of going to the Thanksgiving dinner, he wouldn't have landed his new job – and reacquainted himself with Wendy.

The guys and gals at the office

You spend all day with them, you may as well schmooze with them. Often in the workplace, we don't have time to interact with co-workers much beyond "Why isn't the printer working?" and "Let's do the conference call with Omaha at four o'clock." But does it make sense to divide your life into "daytime work" and everything else? If you choose to live your life seven days a week, then you should get to know the people with whom you may spend more time than anyone else.

First of all, take an interest in your colleagues. Examine their workplaces for evidence of personality, family or hobbies. Many people have pictures of family members or pets in their offices or cubicles. Ask about them, remember their names.

If you want to get beyond the superficialities of workplace contact, you should make an effort to spend time with your co-workers in a non-workplace setting. Even something as simple as walking with a colleague or supervisor to the parking lot will give you time to chat. Suggest you go to lunch, or order takeout from the same restaurant. If your co-workers go for drinks, even if it's at a place you're not normally fond of, try to make an effort to go.

You know them too

Even people who barely know you will probably be receptive, or at least polite, when you approach them. Why haven't they been the ones to come up to you? For one, remember that close to 50 percent of the U.S. population terms themselves shy – a percentage that researchers say is steadily rising. And most people simply aren't willing to expend the time or energy to approach acquaintances. It takes emotional energy to schmooze with people you don't know. The good news is that the more you do, the less energy it takes.

Remember that snobbery has no place in schmoozing. Never assume that someone is not worth schmoozing or is too busy to talk to you. The waitress in your favorite restaurant, your optometrist, your masseuse – all of them are worth chatting with.

How do you schmooze with people you might see once a month? The same way you'd chat with friends or co-workers. If you ask about their kids, what they did that weekend, if they've seen the latest mega-blockbuster movie, you have a much better chance of finding some common ground and connecting. Even a little observation may pick up a detail to be discussed.

Expert schmoozers actually keep records of birthdays, names of children, favorite foods, and other small details that allow them to connect and reconnect with people. Mark down the birthdays of everyone you know on your calendar. Record the ages and names of your acquaintances' kids in your address book. Keep a running record of any noticeable interest or quirk among the people you know. If you happen to run across a news item on one of your friend's industry competitors or an interesting article on paleontology that you just happen to know your doctor's wife would love to read, you can pass it on.

By increasing the frequency and specificity of contact with your acquaintances, you can nudge them up the ladder of relationship closeness. Friendships and contacts aren't created instantly, but through unhurried, amiable schmoozing.

Okay, so you know them, what do you do?

Don't push it

Sometimes, when we're first getting to know someone, we get impatient. Schmoozing – slowly building a relationship – seems slow and frustrating. The important thing is to let connections born of schmoozing develop at their own pace. Is it reasonable to invite someone you've met once to get coffee? Of course. Should you be jealous if your newish acquaintance then fails to invite you to her son's wedding? Of course not. Don't panic if your schmoozing seems to be going slowly. Keep your expectations reasonable, keep schmoozing, and of small beginnings great relationships will be born.

A.J. Benza, the former New York *Daily News* gossip columnist and current E! Entertainment show host, tells us that he's been "lucky in his friends." "I've made contacts" says Benza, "but not the kind of contacts where I'm going to pull on their pants leg and say, hey, can you get me in this movie? If I were that way, I'd be in a lot more films by now. But I've made friends with people who I considered my idols. I'm friends with some of the big names in Hollywood — Jack Nicholson, Warren Beatty, Bob Evans. Those guys are the guys I wanted to be around when I moved out here."

While A.J. Benza considers "Jack" and "Warren" his friends, he exhibits the light touch known to many a good schmoozer. "I'm not going to bother guys like that who are as big as they are, because they're in a position of power and might be able to help me. I wrote a screenplay, but would I put it in Warren's hands? Our friendship would have to be a lot stronger. I'm not going to jeopardize what we have now."

As for the people with whom great relationships don't seem to be forming? "Accept the levels of friendship and closeness among the people you know for what they are," advises Mark Hernandez, our online derivatives trader. That doesn't mean that you can't try to deepen your relationship with your friends and contacts. Just understand that, despite your best schmoozing efforts, not everyone you know will become a valuable ally and friend in exactly the way you want him or her to be. That doesn't mean you should ignore your less-intense relationships. Even if you'll never become soulmates, they are still worth keeping in your schmoozing circle. After all, who knows who they know?

"MEATING" TO SCHMOOZE

You never know when an informal group of friends can turn into an ideal forum for schmoozing. One "prime" example is a group called "The Meateaters." Established in 1992, The Meateaters originally consisted of six recent college grads who met for dinner at the best New York steakhouses, such as Sparks, Peter Luger, and the Post House. It was just like a regular dinner, save for one catch: everyone was required to eat steak, be it sirloin, filet mignon, or prime rib. Explains Meateaters founder N.C. Philips, "In this age of relentless self-denial and obsession with health, it seemed particularly liberating to celebrate the primal joy of spending an evening with a succulent steak."

It turns out that more than a few people shared this passion for porterhouse. Friends of the original founders began attending the dinners, and membership in the group began to grow quickly. The Meateaters soon adopted a formal charter and the policy of granting "Meateaters Membership" only to participants who attended at least four Meateaters' dinners. Full-fledged members received a "Meateaters' Sword": an extra-sharp steak knife engraved with a member's name and the Meateaters logo.

When the ranks of Meateaters surpassed 80 members, it became clear that the group had become something of a schmoozefest. A typical gathering included a diverse mix of Meateaters, from bankers and lawyers to entrepreneurs and grad students to Navy SEALs and budding politicians. The Meateaters began meeting in cities beyond New York, holding their carnivorous court in cities such as San Francisco, Las Vegas, Los Angeles and Boston. The group also spawned offshoot Meateaters groups at Stanford and Harvard Business Schools. Best of all, the Meateaters became known as a place to relax, eat a sumptuous meal, and literally "chew the fat" with like-minded carnivores. "Meateaters fly in from across the country, and sometimes from around the world, to engage in a night of meat-oriented merriment," says Philips. "At every dinner, we try to fulfill the group's mission 'to meat, to vine, to smoke.'"

KEY CONCEPTS

- Don't assume that your closest friends and families know everything that you want and that you know everything about them. Your assumptions may leave hidden certain schmoozing avenues.
- Develop relationships with those you may take for granted — extended family and co-workers.
- Don't be afraid to get back in touch with people.
- Don't push relationships that are just developing.

Susan Molinari

Moral: You can count on your family.

The daughter of longtime U.S. Congressman and current Staten Island Borough President Guy Molinari, Susan Molinari spent her college years partying amiably. Her greatest ambition at the time was to own a bar in the Bahamas. But less that two decades later, the former wild one was giving the keynote address at the Republican National Convention.

Schmooze 'n Spice and everything nice

At the age of 27, Susan decided to take up the family business. In 1985 she ran successfully for City Council. When her father vacated his Congressional seat five years later, leading to a special election, she was strategically placed with a pseudo-incumbent status that helped her to move into the position.

In 1994, when the Republicans took control of the House, Molinari's youth and relative inexperience worked to her advantage during a backlash against politics as usual. A firm pro-choice advocate of women's issues, Molinari stood out against a predominately male, pro-life backdrop of the GOP. Yet her staunch support of Speaker Newt Gingrich kept her in the loop. By 1996, when Republicans were struggling with a candidate that polled poorly with women voters, Bob Dole himself invited Molinari to deliver the keynote address at the Republican Convention. Molinari's bouncy charisma and pro-choice beliefs made her an important player in the party. The convention gave Molinari national exposure.

Molinari profile, cont'd...

But the allure of politics soon paled for Molinari, who decided on a career change. In a gutsy move criticized by both journalists and politicians, she became the first person to go directly from the House to a television anchor position, accepting an offer to host the program, *CBS News Saturday Morning.* Molinari was able to secure the nationally televised program in part because of her experience as a host on a local program, *The Chuck and Sue Show,* which pitted her against then-Democratic Rep. Charles Schumer of Brooklyn in a *Crossfire*-like format. Molinari left *CBS News Saturday Morning* in June 1998 to accept a visiting fellowship at Harvard.

In addition to allowing Molinari more quality time with her daughter and a chance to pay off the three mortgages she shares with her husband, former Republican Congressman Bill Paxon, her new positions have allowed Molinari to increase her public recognition in case (read: probably) she returns to the political arena. By staying true to her feminist beliefs, yet schmoozing both the Republican hierarchy and the worlds of TV news and academia, Molinari's come a long way from her beach bum dreams.

CHAPTER 6

WHO DO THEY KNOW?

The chance encounter

You are in a strange apartment with Danish Modern furniture, a fuzzy green carpet and glossy books, holding a plastic cup that you have recently emptied. You are here with a friend. A colleague from her workplace is having a party. You don't know anyone here except your small knot of acquaintances. What do you do?

First of all, stop looking at the glossy books. Second, enough with the mildly entertaining yet repetitive banter with your friends. Stop being aloof. That Greta Garbo bit may work on the big screen (for Garbo, at least), but not in the real world. You're not in high school anymore, and all those interesting people won't have sixth period English with you every day.

The schmoozer understands that opportunities for a personal connection with a specific person may come more than once – but more often than not, they are like cactus flowers: in full bloom one day, gone the next.

This is a chapter about what we will call secondary contacts – friends of friends, friends of relatives, relatives of friends – and how the schmoozer incorporates them into his or her circle. Although we will examine the dynamics of the friend-of-the-friend interaction in that most notorious of schmoozing situations – the cocktail party – the principles and techniques outlined in this section can be used at any social gathering: professional association dinners, awards banquets, tailgate parties.

"You have the people you know, and that's your first degree," says Andrew Weinreich, founder of an online company that introduces people and their friends to each other. "That's your inner circle — the people you know. A lot of your life is spent just meeting the second degree of people, the people who know the people you know. That's where most of life happens."

Contact

Let's go back to the glossy books and fuzzy green carpet. Your friend is busy chatting with an interesting-looking woman about a stint that woman had with a prominent clothing designer. And damn it, you're looking to get into the fashion industry. Your friend is too entranced to think about you, however – there are no signs of an impending introduction. That's the thing about introductions. Not everyone does them out of habit, and even people who do don't always do them well.

Actually, let's return to a time before the green, shaggy carpet. Let's go back to the car ride, or the leisurely stroll, over to that apartment with the Danish Modern furniture. Remember talking about not assuming that your close friends know everything about you, or you them? This is what we mean. Your friends may feel you are not interested in meeting Joe from work. More likely, the idea of you and Joe meeting will not even cross their minds.

There's an easy way to get this problem out of the way. If you know that your friends will know people at a social function that you do not, ask them about these other attendees. Most people stop with just a cursory assessment of the situation, having gained just enough information to orient themselves: "Okay, I'm going to Sheila's apartment. She's a friend of my friend; they work out at the same gym." That's all they need to know, because they probably plan to hang out with their friends the rest of the evening anyway. A schmoozer, by contrast, finds out more, and more importantly, wants to know more. Schmoozers do their homework.

Research serves the schmoozer well in two ways. First, if you know a little bit about the person, it is easier to build rapport: "So, Sheila tells me you like campy B-movies? Did you see *Revenge of the 90-Foot Transgender Individual,* the sequel to *Attack of the 50-Foot Woman?"* Knowing this information will not alarm your soon-to-be schmoozee, it'll flatter them. It informs the object of your schmoozing that they are worth talking about. Everyone wants to feel important.

Second, casing out personal information lets your friend know that you would like to meet a certain person. "Oh, she sounds really interesting. I'd love to chat with her," the sly schmoozer may remark offhand. "Remember how I told you I wanted to explore options in fashion?" "Hmm," the friend thinks ponderously. "It seems my friend, the B-movie afficionada, also wants to know something about fashion."

Troubleshooting with your buddy

Your friend won't always be the most reliable guide through that cocktail party in the apartment with the fuzzy green carpet. If your pal simply does not like someone, try not to let your primary contact's relationship with that person color your experience. Taking on the burden of another person's dislike is draining and ultimately counterproductive. Your admirable yet misguided loyalty may cause you to prolong a petty vendetta that you have no stake in – even after the original parties have long since made up. Most people will understand if you simply say, "I know you two have had a difficult time, but I'm not involved."

Alternatively, your friend may bump into someone, and be so overcome with joy upon seeing them that you might as well have transmogrified into a non-flowering cactus in the corner (prickly and forlorn). For those times when you're with a friend who is catching up on the last 10 years with someone, listen to your first instincts – give it some time, let them chat. But don't think you're necessarily excluded. If their conversation seems to slow down, simply go and stand by your friend for a minute or two. Your friend should pick up on this and introduce you. If this doesn't immediately work, you can interject with a well-timed: "I'm going to get a drink. Anybody want anything?"

Finally, there are those sticky situations when your friend has run into someone that they can't quite remember. If you sense that your pal is having trouble remembering a name, that's your cue to step up to the plate. Simply stick your hand out and introduce yourself. The other person will respond in kind, and your friend will breathe a big sigh of relief. Maybe later she'll do the same for you.

Exploration

Remember the lessons in Schmoozing 101? They come in especially handy when talking to the people who know the people you know. The first step – finding similarities – is easy enough to do; you've got an acquaintance in common. But the second lesson – figuring out what makes this person interesting, different and fascinating (taking an interest in the person) – sometimes requires verbal leaps across the awkward pregnant silences that follow "So you know Emily."

In other words, you'll want the conversation (and relationship) to evolve to a point where it's no longer dependent on your mutual acquaintance. (After all, you don't forever want to be calling yourself "Emily's brother Barry.") We've already talked about doing "advance scouting" and finding out a little bit about the person before speaking with them. If this can be done, all you really need to do is drop a line like: "So, Emily tells me you're into car detailing..." and take off from there. If no "advance scouting" can be done, a mutual acquaintance can still easily be turned into the starting point for an easygoing conversation – simply ask how they know each other, or if they attended your mutual friend's last birthday party.

SIX DEGREES OF SCHMOOZING

In September 1895, 21-year-old Guglielmo Marconi, a self-taught scientist, performed the first radio communication when he sent a radio-wave signal to his servant three kilometers away. Though Italian authorities dubbed Marconi's newfound technology "not suitable for telecommunications," an era was born. The world, Marconi realized, had just become a smaller place. Marconi, who eventually won a Nobel Prize in Physics for his work, observed that as communication technology continued to evolve, "six degrees of separation" would be all that separated individuals in the modern society. In other words, everyone would be able to reach anyone on earth through six people or less.

And the badass from Bologna couldn't have been more right. In our modern era of phones, beepers, e-mail, web sites, snail mail and fax machines, people are more connected than hot Gummi Bears in a barrel. Marconi's prophecy seems to have come to fruition.

The first study of indirect human connections was undertaken by Harvard social psychologist Stanley Milgram in 1967. Milgram asked subjects in Nebraska and Kansas to mail letters to two people in Boston whom they did not know. The subjects then forwarded a copy of the letter to friends who might know the Boston recipients. On average, the number of people between the random Boston subjects and the Midwesterners was six.

Fast-forward three decades to 1997 and PlanetAll, a Web service designed to help people stay in touch. When members sign up with PlanetAll, they register electronic links with friends and professional contacts with the company. In reviewing its database, PlanetAll found that 97

Six Degrees of Schmoozing, cont'd...

percent of its members were connected by six degrees or less. At the time of its survey, PlanetAll's membership represents more than 50,000 relationships and over 100 countries. The company was acquired by Amazon.com in August 1998.

However, the oddest example of this connective reality is the "Six Degrees of Kevin Bacon" phenomenon.

Started as an amusing accompaniment to beer consumption by three frat boys from the University of Virginia, "Six Degrees of Kevin Bacon" received nationwide recognition for its eerie demonstration of Marconi's prediction. The game consists entirely of mentioning an actor's name and linking it, name by name, back to Cosmic Kev himself. And you thought those two hours you spent watching *Pyrates* were a waste.

The Oracle of Bacon (http://www.cs.virginia.edu/~bct7m/bacon.html) is a web site that lets visitors run names through the Bacon-based search engine. The site shows that even the most unrelated of actors can be traced back to the ubiquitous KB in three links or less. As of November 2000, the Oracle linked 408,220 actors to Bacon. A few examples:

Elvis Presley: The King was in *King Creole* (1958) with Walter Matthau, and Matthau was in *JFK* (1991) with Kevin Bacon.

Ice Cube: The cold one was in *Boyz 'N the Hood* (1991) with Laurence Fishburne, and Fishburne was in *Quicksilver* (1986) with Kevin Bacon.

Bob Hope: The GI's favorite guy was in *The Muppet Movie,* (1979) with Steve Martin, and Martin was in *Planes, Trains & Automobiles* (1987) with Kevin Bacon.

James Dean: The rebel without a reason was in *Giant* (1956) with Barbara Barrie, and Barrie was in *End of the Line* (1987) with Kevin Bacon.

Gary Coleman: Todd Bridges' favorite punching bag was in *On the Right Track* (1981) with Jami Gertz, and Gertz was in *Quicksilver* (1986) with Kevin Bacon.

Evel Knievel: The god of broken bones was in *Viva Knievel!* (1977) with Dabney Coleman, Coleman was in *The Man with One Red Shoe* (1985) with Tom Hanks, and Hanks was in *Apollo 13* (1995) with Kevin Bacon.

What is the student of schmooze to learn from all this? If a pug-nosed character actor from Philly can be linked to every player in his industry, then you're probably a hell of a lot more connected than you think, too. Moral: A schmoozer is not just the sum of his contacts, but the sum of his contacts' contacts also. You never know, reach along your web far enough and you may find a link to the Bacon boy as well. If you do, ask him what the hell he was thinking when he did *Queens Logic.*

The final frontier: drawing secondary contacts in

You've developed rapport with the friend of a friend. You've yukked it up, found some surprising things in common, told some embarrassing secrets, disdained the avocado dip. It's time to leave. Do not go gently into that good night. If you can, try to establish some expectation of future meeting with your new contact.

Try to work with what you've been talking about, if possible – for example, if you've discovered you're both silent movie fans, invite him to the next Valentino retrospective.

Even if it's something you don't think you'll be able to do, set up a meeting. At the very least, if you set something up and have to cancel, you have a reason to call. In fact, correspondence based solely on scheduling and rescheduling between people can last a surprisingly long time. (And, of course, those scheduling and rescheduling conversations can be rife with small chitchat, if not real conversation.) Not that we recommend such a pattern, of course, but if you enjoy each other's company, setting up a meeting for the sake of setting one up is, shall we say, infinitely better than allowing your new acquaintance to slip back into the chasm of the unknown.

Vault Profile: Andrew Weinreich

As a student at the University of Pennsylvania maintaining a significant course load, Andrew Weinreich still found time to start some small businesses. One of them was an SAT prep course which, when sold, funded half of Weinreich's senior year tuition. "There's a very romantic notion about starting businesses in this country," says Weinreich. "I've always found that peoples' interest sparks when you tell them what you're attempting to do and they become incredibly helpful. It's important to tap into that interest." Since then Weinreich founded the once succesful, now defunct web site called sixdegrees.com, a virtual community that allows members to introduce their friends and acquaintances to other contact circles of other members.

How many degrees between you and Andrew?

After Penn, Weinreich joined Merrill Lynch as a financial analyst for a year, before attending Fordham Law School. Weinreich recalls that "law school was a great place to meet people. If you looked hard enough, you could always find someone who could get you where you wanted to go — or at least introduce you to the next link in the chain." Following law school, Weinreich took a job as in-house counsel for pharmaceutical giant Pfizer, but he soon realized he wanted a career in the technology sector.

Weinreich remembers vividly the breakthrough that led to his founding of sixdegrees: "I had a kind of 'Eureka' moment when I realized the real killer app was e-mail and that it would change the way people got in touch with each other." Weinreich also realized that connecting with others would be simpler if the information that connects people could be stored and retrieved. With only those two bits of wisdom, Weinreich was convinced that he had found the way to go. He quit his job, assembled a team, pitched everyone he knew for financing, and started sixdegrees®.

sixdegrees is a Web application based on the theory that we're all connected through a path of no more than six relationships. The company was incorporated in May 1996 and the beta version of the product launched in January 1997. The concept intrigued online schmoozers from the start and membership began accruing immediately. sixdegrees was acquired by YouthStream Media Networks in January 2000 for $125 million.

Schmoozing outside of social events

Planting seeds

Although schmoozers are at their best when casually, blissfully socializing, they know that once in a while, they need something and must tap their circle to attain their particular goal. Expanding their schmoozing circle is the most effective way to attain these goals.

"Look, what is the percentage of people who get jobs through *The New York Times* compared to the people whose dad knows someone somewhere?" says Weinreich of sixdegrees.com. "What is the percentage of people who go to the personal ads to find someone to go out with, compared to the people who have their friends set them up? What is the percentage of people who find an apartment through ads posted on bulletin boards or in the newspaper, and those who find them through friends? It's always the latter."

Your goal is to let your family and friends – your primary contacts – know what's going on in your life and how you can be helped: you need an apartment, a job, a better hairstylist. (By letting them know what's going on in your life, you also let them know how you can help them as well. Good schmoozers are never just takers in a relationship.) Try asking them to "keep their ears open" or to "ask around."

Keep in touch with your primary level of contacts to remind them of your goals and keep them fresh in their minds. This doesn't mean constantly haranguing your friends and family to ask people whether they know anybody that can help you. It's simply a matter of calling to check up and to provide an update on the situation: "Yeah, Jen, I was just calling to see whether anything had popped into your head about my apartment search. I've looked at a couple of places, and I like one of them OK, but I'm not in love with it."

It's also often necessary to keep in touch with your first degree of contact to harvest the fruits of your schmoozing success. Just because your aunt knows somebody who can help you, or may know someone who knows such a person, doesn't mean that she's going to remember to call you about it. The burden of keeping up is on you, not the people nice enough to help you.

Harvest time

Once your cousin tells you that yeah, actually, she has a friend who used to live in San Francisco and can give you advice about apartment-hunting there, and might even have some friends who could hook you up with a place, what do you do?

First of all, don't be daunted by a referral to a stranger. A secondary contact is a powerful thing. Tamara Totah, a headhunter for a New York search firm, explains why she is always willing to take calls from those who simply mention the name of someone she trusts. "I know the guy, I trust him," she says. "He's not going to send me some psycho."

Andre Crump, who has set up an e-mail newsletter for his fellow Kellogg Business School alumni in San Francisco (see profile on p. 258), says finding contacts through the newsletter works regardless of whether the person went to the school. "In a lot of ways it doesn't really matter," he says. "If someone from Kellogg says, 'I know someone who works there' – if it's an alum it's good. If not, it's still good, because it's a friend of a friend."

And don't think that second degree connections must be confined to a region or require a person-to-person introduction. All it really takes is a phone call and a mention of a mutual contact. "If I'm going into a city, I'll drop a call, and say I'm open this evening and that this person said we should meet up for this and this reason," says Bill Demas, a group product manager at Microsoft. "It's not like every time I go into a city, I'm calling everybody and saying, 'Tell me who you know.' It's just if I'm talking to someone who says 'You should talk to my friend,' I'll go ahead and do that."

How to schmooze secondary contacts

You could ask for the phone number of your object of desire, call, and say, "Hi, I'm so-and-so's cousin, and I heard you have friends who might be able to get me an apartment, and can you call them for me?" This could work, and in some cases, will have to do, but this is not the best way to proceed. If you do this, you're relying heavily on your cousin's currency, rather than your own.

"I've had people cold-call me off a list of Stanford alums," says New York freelance writer and producer Lara Rosenthal. "I am always happy to talk to people and give them pointers, and even someone to contact, but if I have met someone I will try more strongly to put them in touch with opportunities."

Moving an initial meeting from a phone conversation to a face-to-face meeting (preferably a social occasion) is key. A schmoozer might host a party, or organize another social event (a tennis match, say, if the schmoozee is a tennis player) and ask the primary contact to invite their pal. Social settings, because they are informal and enjoyable, encourage the conversations and observations at the heart of schmoozing.

A super-schmoozer will deliberately host enticing social events. In 1986, before he started the political commentary program *The McLaughlin Group,* John McLaughlin was the host of a minor program called *One on One.* McLaughlin heard that Charlton Heston and his wife were in Washington and invited them to have dinner with their old friends Ronald and Nancy Reagan – whom he had not yet invited. He invited the Reagans using the Hestons as a drawing card, and vice versa. He also invited the then-chairman of General Electric, Jack Welch, and his wife at the time. At the end of the night, a delighted and star-struck Welch agreed to fund McLaughlin's new TV show.

The other reason meeting referrals face-to-face is important is that it gives you more immediate access to the person and their schmoozing circle. In other words, you'd like the person you are meeting to give you more names. You aren't just interested in your cousin's friend's knowledge of apartments in San Francisco, but the other people they know who might also know how to get apartments.

Andy Weinreich of sixdegrees.com stresses that contacts are generally accessible if they are only "two degrees" away. Thus the important step to keeping the schmoozing machine churning is turning secondary contacts into primary contacts – the last step in our cocktail party scenario. "Some stuff does happen in a third-degree way," Weinreich says. "For example, someone who works with your mom is married to someone in a company you want to work for. Your responsibility then is to meet your mom's co-worker and make her a first-degree contact. Then her husband is a second-degree contact."

Without converting distant contacts into people personally known to you, the power of going through friends of friends of friends eventually diminishes, Weinreich says. "Fourth-degree is pretty tenuous and there are diminishing returns," he says. "After fifth, it doesn't really matter. I mean, I may know Bill Clinton through five people, but he's not going to take my calls."

Taking off

Second-degree schmoozing can bring unexpected benefits. Suzanne Turk, a flight attendant for Atlantic Southeast Airlines who lives in Dallas, often recognizes her frequent flyers and develops personal relationships with them. "I'll just remember their favorite drink, they'll recognize me, we'll talk. I've had dinner with passengers during layovers, and I've dated some as well," she says.

"Once I was chatting with someone and it turned out he worked at Pfizer, the major drug company," she says. "I had a friend who was a pharmaceutical representative and was looking for a new position. I mentioned this, and he gave me his card and told me to tell my friend to give him a call," she says. "Now she works at Pfizer."

KEY CONCEPTS

- Make sure your circle knows that you want to meet the people they know.
- Use mutual contacts as a starting point to build rapport.
- Understand the power of a secondary contact.
- After getting a referral, try to meet that person in a social situation.
- Keep the cycle going — get referrals from those you meet.

CHAPTER 7

HEY, WHO'S THAT?

Schmoozing beyond the basics

In the last chapter we advanced from the cliché of the mutual-friend meeting place, the cocktail party, to that laboratory of stranger interaction, the airport. In this chapter, we'll continue to use airports as the model for examining meetings of strangers. Then, we'll turn our attention to approaching specific people.

But, you may say, the last two chapters were all about schmoozing people I knew, and the folks they knew. How am I supposed to talk to strangers? Nonsense. Remember what we said at the beginning of the "The Schmoozer's Mindset"? Everybody you know was once a stranger.

Bridgett Bailee, our former Mary Kay director in San Antonio, often finds potential customers and employees among the people she meets by chance. "I found that I met customers and potential consultants just by talking to people. I'm always smiling at people and if they smile back, I'll talk to them," says Bailee. "If I'm in an airport, I'll talk about the flight we're waiting for, or I'll ask them where they're going. Small talk like that gets you through people's comfort zone and they are willing to tell you more."

Position yourself

Let's say that you, too, are at the airport. Your goal as a public schmoozer is to make sure you don't blend into the scenery. Often when we're alone in a public place, we take little notice of the people around us. How to make contact? You might offer gum for the ascent, notice what they're reading and make some kind of comment on it (though try to be positive – "John Grisham sure sucks" isn't the best icebreaker if your seatmate happens to be a rabid fan of the novelist). You can even ask for assistance with your own bags (though it helps if you actually need it). Basically, you want to break through their complacency – become a person and not just someone to climb over on the way to the bathroom.

Starting the conversation

HANDY CONVERSATION STARTERS

At a large event
"What brings you here?"

At cinema or theater
"What else have you seen recently?" or "I love (whoever's) work."

At business event
"What affiliation do you have with the company?"

At bookstore
"Have you read anything by this author?"

At an airport, highway rest stop or bus terminal
"Where are you headed?"

Anywhere
"Isn't it the most beautiful/rainy/foggy/chilly day? How unusual for this time of the year!"

The rules of starting conversations are simple – if you're willing to take a chance and follow them. First of all, suggests Kathryn Dindia, the communications professor, simply make eye contact. When this initial bond is forged, smile and say hello. "That's it," reports Dindia. "There have been studies of opening lines, and which work better than others, but you don't need to be creative. Just make eye contact, and then, just 'hi' will work."

Once you've said your hellos, however, you still have work to do. You must make an opening comment, or, as Dindia puts it, "you'll just stand around feeling like idiots with nothing to talk about." Instead, pick any common experience: "Comments about weather or the slowness of elevators are very common openers," Dindia says.

Vault Profile: Fiona Smith

Growing up, freelance photographer and writer Fiona Smith thought her father suffered from what she terms acute "diarrhea of the mouth." When they traveled together as a family, she and her brother would squirm as her father struck up conversations with anyone and everyone within arm's reach: people in elevators, in restaurants, on buses, on airplanes, or while waiting in line. As a kid, it embarrassed her to no end. But today she refers to him as a champion schmoozer. What changed? Certainly not her father. He's still the same schmoozing guru he has always been. It was Fiona herself who changed. From watching her father, she realized that there are certain perks that come with schmoozing. For one thing, strangers treat you better because they feel as if they know you.

photo by Paula Singer

Fiona Smith

Don't worry, be confident

"Many people are fearful of how they will look if they approach strangers and start up a conversation with them," says Smith. Her philosophy is that there may a be lot of things to be afraid of in this world, but that talking to people shouldn't be one of them.

To be a successful schmoozer, Smith recommends you be genuinely curious about other people. It's also important that you be perceptive and cultivate an extroverted personality. For those not possessed of a naturally effervescent demeanor, Smith offers these tips.

Three rules of schmooze

1. You can always learn something from everyone you meet. Curiosity about other people is the first and foremost quality of a schmoozer. You cannot be a decent schmoozer if you do not have a genuine interest in learning about the other person.

2. Keep your eyes open. A student of the world, Smith is fascinated by all things cultural and international. Whenever she meets people who have an accent or who look like they might have an international background, she asks where they're from. "Chances are," she says, "that from my avid reading about places around the world, I am able to say a few intelligent things about the person's country. You would be surprised how many friends I have made through my passion for the world."

3. Don't relegate schmoozing to work. Smith refers to herself as a day-to-day schmoozer, indicating that schmoozing is something that should be practiced and lived in everyday life.

Bad schmoozing

People who give one-word answers are perennially bad schmoozers. The same goes for people who can only talk about work. Other advice for wannabe-schmoozers? "Don't come on too strong because people will tell you more if you are non-threatening and mellow," says Smith. "[Be] yourself, because people do not like talking to someone who is insincere and fake. Have a sense of humor — people love to laugh and think that they are funny."

Party of one

Smith is the type of person who embraces the anxiety and challenge of going to a party stag, if just to be reminded that people don't bite and that it's fun to go into a room full of strangers and emerge with a few potential friends.

"Many people do not feel comfortable going to a party by themselves because they are fearful of looking desperate to meet people because they are alone," she says. "This is not a valid fear ... people are basically skin, bones, and a few organs with a personality. Since we are social beings, we like interaction with other human beings. Whenever I cannot find a friend to go to a party with me I look at the party as a social challenge."

But how are you supposed to know what you have in common with a stranger? You don't know who your fellow passengers are, or even where they are from. All you know is that you're all sitting in the same waiting lounge, looking over whatever book or magazine you've culled from the newsstand, and that soon you'll be on the same airborne vessel for the next four or five hours, eating roasted peanuts out of little foil packs and cajoling the flight attendant into leaving you the entire can of soda. Wait a second, that's an entire experience in common!

Don't take it personally

Schmoozing isn't always successful, at least at first, and the good schmoozer should be careful to respect limits when approaching strangers. Rob, a recent college graduate in Virginia, once attempted to schmooze a man wearing the sweatshirt of his alma mater in an airport lounge. But the man barely uttered a word in response to Rob's friendly overtures. Later, Rob ended up sitting next to the man. Rob smiled at the man but made no other attempts at conversation. Finally, when the plane had taken off, the man ordered a Scotch and soda from the flight attendant, turned to Rob, and apologized. It turned out the man was terrified of flying and had been physically unable to speak until the plane was safely in the air. Still, don't push it. If the current apple of your schmoozing eye seems reluctant, or tired, or just unfriendly, gracefully disengage. The person's reluctance to chat most likely has nothing to do with you.

Give everyone a schmoozing chance

Marla, our political consultant from "True Tales of Schmoozing Success," makes it a point to schmooze anyone, anywhere. She finds airplanes a perfect opportunity to practice her schmoozing talents. "When I first get on an airplane, I immediately introduce myself to my seatmate. I just say "Hi, I'm Marla," we shake hands, and chat a little bit, maybe about where we're from or whether we're traveling for business or pleasure or whatever. Then, I'll give them a little while to settle in or whatever, and then we'll talk the rest of the flight." But Marla, what if the person next to you just doesn't want to talk, or is rude to you? "That rarely happens, but if someone is rude to me, I will ask the stewardess for a seat change. In general, though, I find that once you start talking to people, they are very pleasant and helpful."

Putting nervousness aside

Bridgett Bailee's former employer, Mary Kay Cosmetics, has a term for conversations with newly met people – "warm chattering." "We tell people, 'You're not talking to a stranger, you're meeting a new friend,'" Bailee relates. "I am always running into people I meet that I like," she adds. "They will often ask what I do, or I'll bring it up, and I tell them what I do at Mary Kay and they usually get very interested. I meet people everywhere. I'll meet them in the grocery store or restaurants. You just must always be open to meeting people."

Vault Profile: J. Owen Todd

It is said of prominent Boston lawyer J. Owen Todd that he is unable to leave a cocktail party without picking up a client. Todd, a former Superior Court judge in Massachusetts, says he has derived his social ability largely from his professional ability. Of the ability to schmooze, he says "perhaps it is synonymous with self-confidence. It develops as one's career develops – I think that was true in my case."

Permission to schmooze, your honor

It is unlikely Todd ever was lacking in confidence. A Boston native, he attended Harvard College, went to law school nearby at Boston College, and joined the prestigious law firm of Hale and Dorr. Todd eventually made senior partner at Hale and Dorr and helped recruit former Massachusetts Governor Bill Weld into the firm before becoming a judge. A father of four, Todd resigned from the Superior Court so he could practice law with his son. He is now a partner in the firm of Todd and Weld (not that Weld).

Todd is a firm believer that sociability can be learned. He points to his son, Gary, as a prime example, and notes that Gary became more social as late as his last year of law school.

"When I was a judge, Gary would come to court and be introduced to the judges, and meet the Governor, and would see that they weren't so awful, just regular folks, not people to be feared," Todd says. "I had him work on a political campaign in order to appreciate that little people are as important as big people, and that big people are not unique. He's much more comfortable with and interested in meeting people now."

Communicating with people big and little is an important part of how Todd views being a trial lawyer. "I really get very excited when I enter a room and see an awful lot of people and among them, persons that I know very well, and persons that I'd like to know ... I really get charged up and think it's going to be very, very interesting."

Unlike other master schmoozers, Todd doesn't spend a great deal of energy collecting business cards or keeping track of people he's met. His poor memory for names (although not for faces), is a running joke in the Boston legal community. "I don't care if I remember the names, in fact I usually don't," he says. Todd thinks it really doesn't matter. "As long as you show that you are interested, remembering names doesn't matter."

"I'll always say, 'Yes, the name isn't coming to me,' or 'I'm having a senior moment about your name,'" he says. Todd has another standard way of getting around his name forgetfulness. "I just call everybody 'my friend,'" he says.

Not only does J. Owen Todd, a lawyer in Boston, not feel nervous about approaching strangers, he says he gets very excited about meeting new people at parties and professional association meetings. "If they're alone, I'll just go up to them and say, 'It's a great party, isn't it? Are you enjoying yourself? What do you do? Are you a lawyer?' and just start a conversation that way," Todd says. "If they're in groups, I might say, 'Gee, I think it's interesting that somebody said this...'"

Keeping in touch

We'll talk more about keeping in touch in the next chapter, but following up with a person you've just met is especially important. For starters, you can't depend on bumping into the person again, and you can't ask your friends about the person, as you might with "the people they know" – you need to be able to know how to keep in touch.

Cards with your name, phone number, e-mail address, regular address and organization are always a useful schmoozing tool when meeting strangers. That way, when you meet someone and would like to continue to keep in touch, you can exchange cards as a fast way to get contact information. (At the very least, a business card allows you to enter all those free-lunch drawings at local restaurants.)

How to exchange cards? The best thing to do is say something like "I've enjoyed talking with you. Is there any chance you have a card I could take?" After taking the card, you should give your schmoozee your own card. As soon as you get the card, write some sort of mnemonic device on it, like "Rides horses" or "Loves to travel." (Try not to do this in front of the person, especially if the key to your memory is something like "bad dye job.")

But what if you don't have a business card, or if your conversation partner doesn't have one? That's where a little address book or Filofax comes in handy. You can simply take down your new acquaintance's appropriate information. Write a little note next to the person's name. We advise that you make some sort of suggestion about meeting in the future that is reasonably precise. "Let's have lunch," is too vague, but "I'll be in your part of town for a meeting Thursday after next. Why don't we have breakfast?" is specific. Even if the person can't meet you then, he or she is more likely to suggest an alternative.

Make sure you follow up. Especially perfect for follow-up schmoozing is e-mail – a quick note dashed off to let your new acquaintance know how much you enjoyed meeting him, recapping a few things you talked about, is easy and greases the wheels for later schmoozing.

Targeted schmoozing: meeting someone specific

Have a reason to contact them

Maybe you just want to schmooze with someone in particular, but you don't really know how. What if you'd like to meet the CEO of your company? Or one of your favorite authors? It can be done. But first, you need to get in touch with your target. And second, you have to have something to say.

David Nowakowski, a 28-year-old student at the London School of Economics, was at a party with his friend when he saw the actress Sigourney Weaver. David approached her, not with requests for an autograph but with a question about *Death and the Maiden*, a lesser-known movie in which she acted. As Nowakowski tells the story, he was settling into a pleasant conversation when his friend walked up and asked, "When's the next *Aliens* coming out?" "She started looking around and then said, 'I have to go,' and left," he recounts sadly.

Explains Nowakowski, "I think I was just hoping she'd be nice. I thought about what I was going to say." But the savvy Nowakowski had three things he was prepared to talk about: *Death and the Maiden*; *Annie Hall* (in which Weaver had a bit part); and as a third and last option, the *Aliens* movies. He explains he didn't want to talk about the *Aliens* series, because "she's probably not that proud of it, although *Alien* is a great movie." But this anecdote is instructive not because we need to learn that one shouldn't ask stupid questions when talking to famous movie actresses. It's instructive because we need to understand that anybody can be approached with the appropriate respect and curiosity.

Nowakowski credits his optimism for his willingness to approach strangers like Weaver. "I tell myself there's nothing really bad that's going to happen. At worst, I'll make a fool of myself temporarily," he maintains. "Sometimes I don't do it, and then I regret it. After enough times that you've missed opportunities, you realize that the downside is not anything that bad. You forget about it and move on."

Nowakowski was not always comfortable approaching strangers and would probably have been considered shy by his friends in college. "I've learned that schmoozing is fun," he says. "It's a little adventure, and sometimes there's something to be gained." A schmoozer is curious. A schmoozer sees opportunity where others see strangers.

Vault Interview: Rob Nelson, Founder, Lead...or Leave

In 1992 Rob Nelson co-founded Lead...or Leave, the first national 'Generation X' political organization in the U. S. By 1995 the organization had become the largest such group in the country with 30,000 members, chapters in all 50 states, and a college network that spanned 150 universities. The year it was founded, Lead...or Leave got more than 100 Congressional candidates to pledge to cut the deficit. In later years, it helped spark a national political debate around Social Security reform, in part by holding the first-ever rally in support of reforming the system. In just over two years Lead...or Leave raised close to $2 million and organized more than 250 rallies.

Lead, Leave... or Schmooze!

As the organization grew, Nelson was featured on the cover of magazines such as U.S. News & World Report *and in publications such as* Time, Newsweek, *and* The New York Times. *He was a featured guest on programs such as* Nightline, Politically Incorrect, *the* Today Show, *and* Crossfire *with Pat Buchanan and Michael Kinsley. Nelson was a guest on* Good Morning America *three times. In 1994 Nelson and Lead...or Leave co-founder Jon Cowan wrote* Revolution X, *a generational political mainfesto published by Penguin with a forward by then-New Jersey Senator Bill Bradley. Since his Lead...or Leave days, Nelson has been quite busy. He graduated from Stanford Law School and wrote another book,* Last Call: 10 Common-Sense Solutions to America's Biggest Problems *(published in February 2000). He currently hosts a nationally-syndicated talk show on the Fox network called* The Rob Nelson Show.

Nelson interview, cont'd...

Lead...or Leave's prominence brought Nelson into contact with a wide variety of politicians and celebrities. The organization's advisory board included Lee Iacocca, the late Texas Congresswoman Barbara Jordan, and the late Massachusetts Senator Paul Tsongas, then-Governors Bill Weld (of Massachusetts) and Ann Richards (of Texas), and actors Val Kilmer and Christian Slater. Vault caught up with Nelson to talk about approaching such luminaries with his idea. He told us about being persistent in contacting people – and then he told us about approaching people while they're checking their mail.

Vault: In referring to your efforts founding Lead...or Leave, *Time* magazine suggested that you were a consummate twentysomething schmoozer. Do you agree?

Nelson: I'm not a smooth talker who calculates his next move and creates lists of people to speak to. What I do is identify people I want to reach out to. I use my intuition.

Vault: What is the most important trait to be a successful schmoozer in D.C.?

Nelson: My attitude is that people can smell a bad schmoozer a mile off. They see you coming and just put up walls. What really helped me get in the door was believing in what I was doing. If you're not passionate about something, then it's just not worth doing. But if you totally believe in what you're talking about, then it gives you the power to pursue something doggedly and with great enthusiasm. The key is to knock on every single door. Become immune to rejection. People will blow you off again and again, but someone will listen.

Vault: Give me an example of how you pursued something in this fashion.

Nelson: Well, when my partner Jon [Cowan] and I were starting Lead...or Leave, we tried to contact [the late presidential candidate] Paul Tsongas but he would not return our calls. So we called his secretary twice a day until she got so frustrated that she finally put him on the phone.

Vault: What are some other keys to schmoozing in D.C.?

Nelson: Don't try to schmooze the world, just a select few. This applies anywhere, but especially in D.C. The key is to pick a handful of people and let them know, "I need your help reaching other people." One linked person can lead you to 10 or even 50 other people. For example, once we got Ross Perot to support Lead...or Leave, he was willing to call a few of his powerful friends and say, "I agreed to help these guys, and

Nelson interview, cont'd...

I want you to help them too." The great thing is that this just took 10 minutes of Perot's time.

Vault: What makes an unsuccessful schmoozer?

Nelson: Someone who crosses the line and does not know when to ease off. This happened to me at the MTV Inaugural Ball. I approached Jack Nicholson about getting involved in Lead...or Leave, and he was in no mood to talk about helping a twentysomething political activist group. I got in his face, was really blunt, and pissed him off. I should have been less direct.

Vault: It seems like "network building" was elemental to the success of Lead...or Leave. How did schmoozing pay off for the organization?

Nelson: We built a national circle of people who thought like we did. Because it was so clear what we stood for, it was easy to get people involved... so many people saw it and related. We had an advisory board which had everyone from CEO Lee Iacocca to Democratic Governor Ann Richards to Republican Governor Bill Weld to '60s activist Tom Hayden to actor Christian Slater. We built this organization that spanned such different political agendas because we were able to invest everyone in the process, regardless of their ideological beliefs.

Vault: Do you have any other advice for budding schmoozers?

Nelson: You need to be flexible and ready to seize opportunities. One example is when my partner and I were driving in a car and saw [*Washington Post* reporter] David Broder walking to a mailbox. Without hesitation, we drove our car to the curb, jumped out, and starting talking to him about Lead...or Leave. He ended up writing a great article on the organization. Here's another example – in the first weeks of running Lead...or Leave, Val Kilmer saw us on CNN and called our office to tell us he liked what we were doing. Instead of just thanking him and letting him go, I invested him in what we were doing. I asked him to do the voiceover for a Lead...or Leave television commercial, and he agreed. He ended up introducing us to some key people in Hollywood who helped us build a critical network in the entertainment community. He enjoyed working with our organization and liked our mission. He also agreed to serve on Lead...or Leave's advisory board. It all goes back to getting people invested in what you're doing.

Write a letter

Everyone loves mail. That includes busy executives, celebrities and, most of all, those men and women of letters, authors. If someone you admire has written a book, write him or her a letter about it. It is best in these letters to be extremely specific about what you liked and did not like, and what questions you have. Note-sized letters are even more likely to be looked at, as they don't blend in with the regular junk mail. Include your e-mail address in the letterhead. This is especially good because if your target decides to respond, you can start a dialogue via e-mail. Many magazine and newspaper writers include their e-mail address at the end of their articles, practically begging for correspondence.

THE POWER OF LETTER-WRITING

Ol' Dale Carnegie, of *How to Win Friends and Influence People*, boasts in his famous tome about all the fabulous people he's met through simply writing them a letter. Now, understand that as many letters as you write, you probably still won't chat with people as famous as Herbert Hoover, as Carnegie did. Still, a simple letter to a celebrity can have surprising results. Samantha Smith, a fifth-grader from Maine, sent a letter to Soviet leader Yuri Andropov at the height of the Cold War, asking him to explain his strategy for avoiding a war between the USSR and the United States. Andropov sent Samantha a telegram, inviting her to visit the Soviet Union and make her own decisions about the country. Samantha spent a highly publicized two weeks inside the then-Communist country. When asked after her tour whether she still believed Andropov would start a war, the bright-eyed preteen answered happily, "Oh, no!" her fears settled after her two-week junket through America's then-adversary.

Top executives George Bell, the chairman of Excite@Home, and Jane Pratt, editor of her eponymous *Jane* magazine, confirm that even the busy and famous will take the time to read a well-written, targeted letter. "If I think someone has done their homework and will run with the advice I give them," Pratt tells us, "sure, I'll take the time out to talk to them. While I get a lot of mail, very little of it concerns career advice."

Your mail should have content other than a mere expression of admiration. Asking for advice or clarification about something your schmoozee has said or done is a better way to get a response and open the doors of communication. Still "almost no one takes the trouble to write," according to airplane-savvy Marla. "Just by writing a letter, you've already set yourself apart from the vast majority of people out there."

The Daisy Fuentes Rule

John Schenk, the chef/owner of the swank Clementine restaurant in downtown New York, tells Vault his rule for serving celebrities.

"We have the Daisy Fuentes rule now. When you first open up a restaurant, we get lots of people in the restaurant business – chefs, waiters, managers – and of course, the stars. Everyone was getting something for nothing. But for some reason, we were being really standoffish when it came to stars. So one day I was in the kitchen and Daisy Fuentes came into the restaurant. I said, damn it, send Daisy Fuentes a second course! So we did and she loved it. Now we always send something to people we recognize. I like to know when celebrities are in my restaurant.

At the same time, I'm against the starf---er restaurant. It can work at some level, but really you have to treat everyone with respect. Everyone wants a little free thing in a restaurant. Everyone wants to be left alone. We once had Tori Spelling come in, and people were literally coming in from the bar and staring at her. We had to shoo people away. But then that guy, who played the nut from *Seinfeld,* Kramer, he loves to work the room, you can't shut him up. Basically, in a restaurant business, it's just a matter of knowing when to say no to people, which you do rarely."

Warren Buffett, one of the best investors of our time, got a head start with a simple letter. He'd been rejected by Harvard Business School and started researching other business institutions. While reading Columbia's catalogue, he noticed that David Dodd, whose book *Security Analysis* he had read and enjoyed, was a teacher and associate dean at Columbia. He sat down and wrote Dodd a letter, expressing his admiration and explaining his situation. Buffett enrolled at Columbia the next month, and Dodd served as mentor for his budding career.

Find out where they are going to be. Be there.

If you know, for example, that the CEO of your company comes into work at the ungodly hour of 5:45 a.m., you might want to show up then for a few weeks. If there are few other people around, Mr. CEO will no doubt take notice of you. Michael Bloomberg, the founder of Bloomberg News Service and current mayor of New York City, credits part of his career success to his development of relationships with the top folk at Salomon Brothers. How did he develop those relationships? As told in his autobiography, *Bloomberg by Bloomberg*, the future media king arrived at the office at 7 a.m. when only "Billy Salomon," (managing partner William R. Salomon) was around: Bloomberg talked sports with the top dog. Bloomberg also stayed late, thus getting the chance to schmooze with Salomon Brothers' No. 2 man, John Gutfreund, while sharing cab rides.

Novelist Mat Johnson points out that one good way to meet authors and other celebrities is to go to book readings and lectures. But instead of waiting until after the reading and approaching with the other 50 fans and acolytes after the speech, Johnson advises arriving early. "Often the lecturer will be standing around with nothing to do," says Johnson, who has schmoozed with authors like Toni Morrison and Caryl Phillips and who once got a job as a writer's assistant after meeting an author at a book reading. "It's the perfect time to approach. Wish them luck, chat a little bit about the speech. Then go say "hi" after the lecture. They'll be happy to see a familiar face."

Price Hicks, the director of education at the Academy of Arts & Sciences, meets people under similar circumstances: "The time I always have with celebrities is in the makeup room. Some of them want to chat – about the show, about themselves, and about you. I always go into the makeup room and ask them if they need anything."

Another technique — ask the lecturer for his or her business card. They may be accustomed to signing autographs, but the request for a card, in a sense, puts you on the same level. If they do give you their business card, hand them yours as well. "Another terrific method of meeting people is to volunteer for an organization's speaker's committee," says Johnson. "Then be the one to pick the speaker up at the airport. You can get someone alone in the car for nearly an hour. You have unparalleled access."

Take notice of openings to meet with your intended schmoozee. If that CEO you admire is giving a speech at a local university, or a politician is having a fundraising dinner you're able to attend, make sure you're there. Or if a celebrity you would like to meet happens to work with the Cystic Fibrosis Foundation, you could volunteer to help organize an event. Be respectful, say what you want to say, and try to make a good impression in the amount of time you have. Don't fawn, don't giggle, don't get nervous.

Just remember that everyone, no matter how well-known, is human. Just like you shouldn't assume that anyone is beneath your schmoozing radar, you shouldn't assume that anyone is too lofty to be schmoozed. "It's a small world," says Marla, our political consultant. "Everyone schmoozes everyone else. You can get to, and talk to, anyone out there in the world."

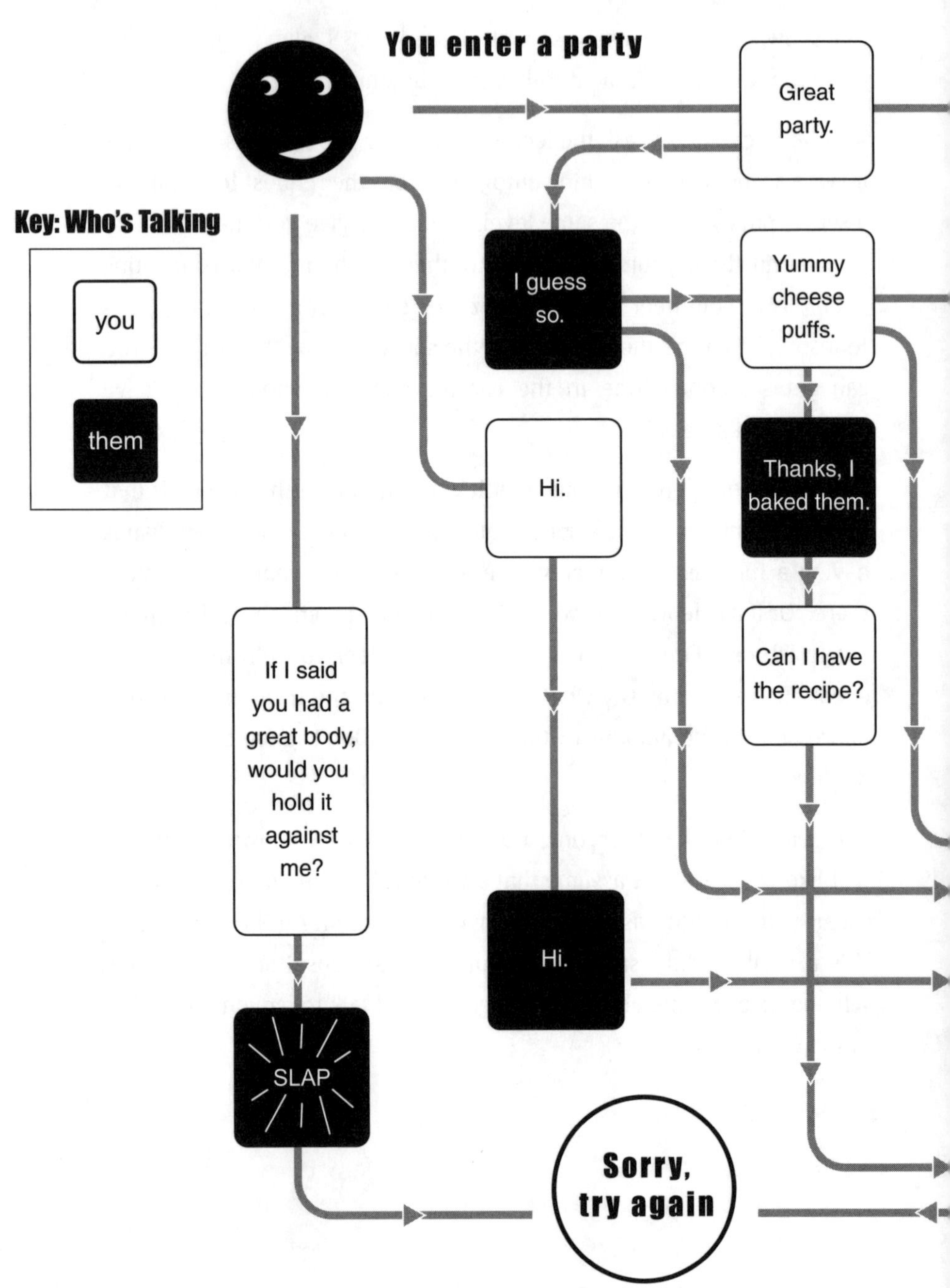
You enter a party
Key: Who's Talking
you
them
Great party.
I guess so.
Yummy cheese puffs.
Hi.
Thanks, I baked them.
Can I have the recipe?
If I said you had a great body, would you hold it against me?
Hi.
SLAP
Sorry, try again

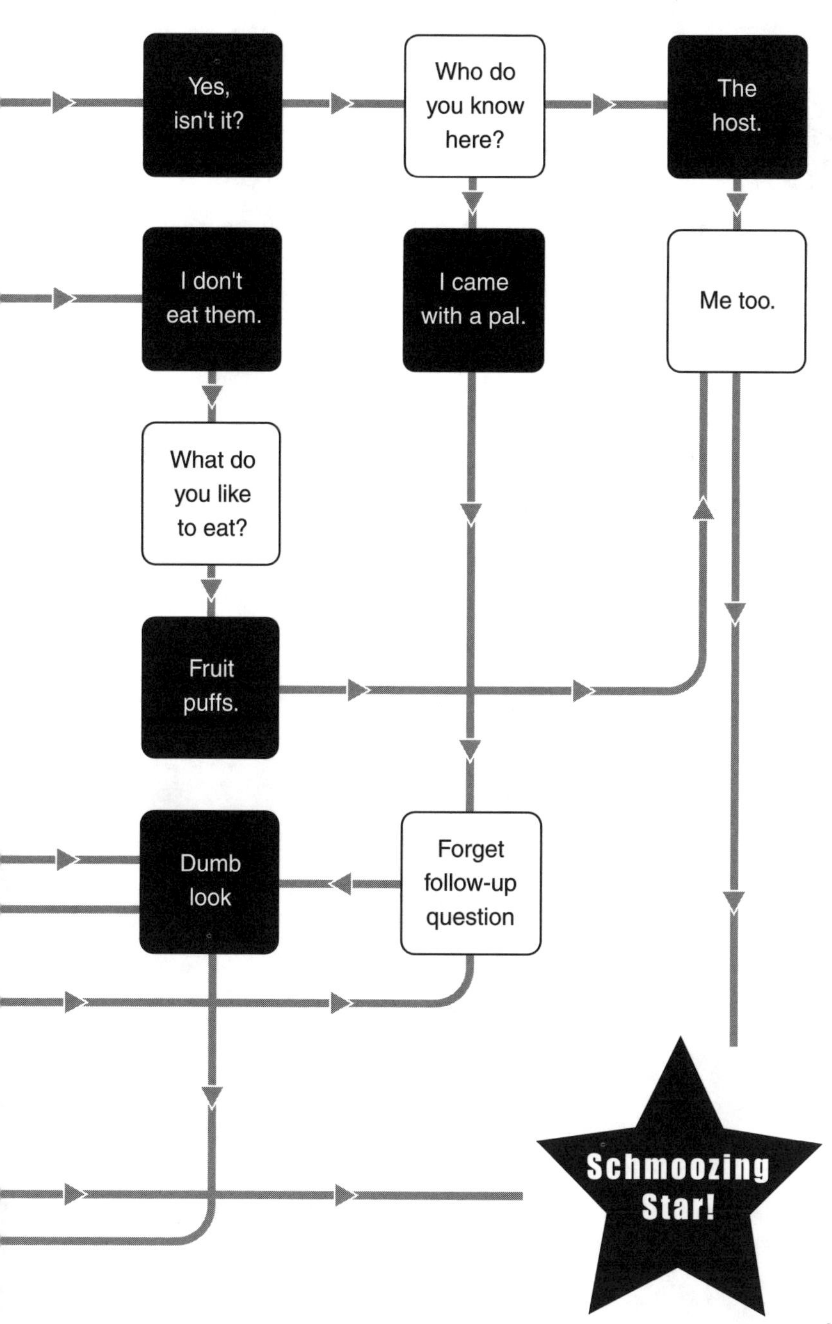
Yes,
isn't it?
Who do
you know
here?
The
host.
I don't
eat them.
I came
with a pal.
Me too.
What do
you like
to eat?
Fruit
puffs.
Dumb
look
Forget
follow-up
question
Schmoozing
Star!

KEY CONCEPTS

- Take a genuine interest in the people you meet.
- Remember that everyone can be approached – no one is out of your league.
- Write letters.
- Arrive early at events.
- Seize the schmoozing moment.

Presidents: Hail to the Schmoozer

1. **Bill Clinton** — Even nemesis Newt Gingrich admits that he has to like the guy. A masterful combination of Southern charm, intense focus on the object of schmoozing, and incredible stamina for keeping in touch with contacts.

2. **JFK** — Telegenic, schmoozy JFK hobnobbed with the Hollywood stars, maybe the mafia, and exuded an overall charm that continues to cause historians to overlook his many foibles.

3. **Teddy Roosevelt** — At a time when White House servants were passed on from administration to administration, Roosevelt took the time to learn their first names, ask them about their corn bread recipes, and call them to tell them that pretty birds were perched outside their windows. The hunting and traveling enthusiast also had a ready store of anecdotes used to regale diplomats and common folk alike.

4. **Ronald Reagan** — The great communicator. He was an actor, after all.

5. **Harry Truman** — He hopped around the country by train, meeting people endlessly, to pull off the great upset against Dewey. The epitome of indefatigable schmoozing.

6. **John Quincy Adams** — Lots of people (well, a good many) had presidents as fathers. Also knew how to play the tit-for-tat game, naming Henry Clay as his secretary of state after the powerful representative threw his support behind Adams in a party run-off.

7. **FDR** — With his fireside chats, the only president to be elected to four terms calmed the American public and steadied a shaky ship.

8. **Taft** — Even as president, he went right on schmoozing, landing himself a spot on the Supreme Court after his term was up.

9. **Abraham Lincoln** – You don't go from log cabin to White House without being able to schmooze. Honest and succinct, Lincoln was known as much for his congenial country wit as his political savvy.

10. **George Washington** – Even without teeth, he was able to pull a country together. Also knew not to overstay his welcome, leaving after two terms.

Lame Duck Schmoozers

1. **Richard Nixon** — "Tricky Dick" was not only so paranoid that he broke the law to ensure an election that was in the bag already, but years earlier he drowned the TV cameras with his sweat during his debates with Kennedy.
2. **Warren Harding** — He depended on his cronies — his "kitchen cabinet" — instead of continuing to expand his circle of advisors. The result? The Teapot Dome Scandal.
3. **Calvin Coolidge** — His nickname was 'Silent Cal.' At one dinner party, a woman waged a bet that she could make Silent Cal say three words. She approached the president and told him about the bet. Cal replied, "You lose," and remained mute the rest of the evening.
4. **Ulysses S. Grant** — Hitting the bottle: perhaps good for war, bad for political schmoozing.
5. **William Henry Harrison** — Harrison talked so long at his inauguration that he developed pneumonia from the outdoors exposure of the ceremony and died after serving only one month in office. He should have listened more, like a good schmoozer.
6. **Gerald Ford** — Golfing does not equal schmoozing. Never really had to schmooze the masses: he and George W. Bush were the only presidents never to be popularly elected.
7. **Millard Filmore** — Who's that? Exactly. Maybe if he had schmoozed a little more, we'd know who he was.
8. **Herbert Hoover** — Spent his last days in office hiding in the White House.
9. **George Bush** — Just ask anyone at a Japanese banquet.
10. **Andrew Johnson** — Unable to appease the Southern Democrats enough to prevent himself from becoming impeached. And it didn't even take an intern.

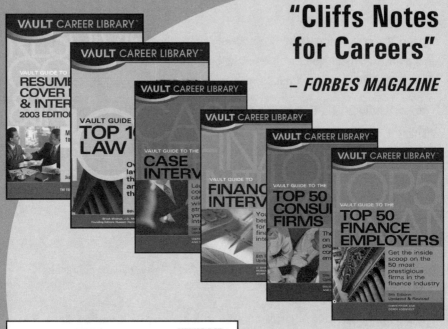

CHAPTER 8

SCHMOOZING 102: STAYING IN TOUCH

Pity the chipmunk

Establishing a schmoozing contact is like hatching sea monkeys. Nurture them, and they proliferate. But forget to feed them, and they'll fade away to nothingness. Many potential schmoozers make good starts at establishing fruitful relationships but forget that maintenance and cultivation of schmoozing circles is just as important as initial contact. People don't like to be pushy, and so we have a tendency to give up too early and scurry away like chipmunks back to our own lives, ready to feast on whatever information or favors we've come across in the first foray into schmoozing.

Are you a chipmunk? Once you have breakfast with that sister of a work colleague, or call up that nice woman you met in the restaurant, are you shy about pursuing the relationship further? "I already got that person to meet me," thinks the typical chipmunk, gnawing away at the single personal contact it's obtained. "She doesn't want to meet with me again. I'll be bothering her. God, I hate bothering people."

Having served as a mentor through the National Society of Fundraising Executives, New York fundraiser Juliet Gumbs says she often witnessed the scared chipmunk phenomenon. "I've sat down with five people to mentor, and only one will call you back, even though you tell them it's fine. People don't believe that you mean it."

Wicke Chambers, the communications consultant from Atlanta, tells similar tales of here-today, gone-tomorrow chipmunks. "I am on the board of trustees at the University of Georgia, and I was approached by a senior during a school event," she says. "He told me he had been trying to get a call-back from some people he had worked with. I knew about a similar job at a bank, and I gave him some contacts there. But he never called me back. I really would have loved to have heard what was going on. If he had told me either way I would have helped him again."

Help you once, help you again

Robert Cialdini in his landmark book, *Influence, the Psychology of Persuasion,* identifies the human need for consistency as one of the major motivating forces of human behavior. To open his discussion of consistency, Cialdini cites an experiment which showed that when polled, bettors at a racetrack were more confident about their choices immediately after placing a bet than immediately before. Once they've made a decision, the experiment suggests, people naturally arrange their thinking so it supports their choice.

This human craving for consistency is illustrated perfectly in an experiment performed by psychologists Jonathan Freedman and Scott Fraser and cited by Cialdini. In the mid-1960s, the pair asked California homeowners whether they would be willing to have an ungainly billboard installed on their front lawns reading DRIVE CAREFULLY, showing residents a picture of an attractive house blocked by a sign with poor lettering.

They divided their unwitting subjects into two groups. One group was asked two weeks earlier to display a three-inch square sign that said BE A SAFE DRIVER (the vast majority agreed to this trivial request); the other group was not. The commitment that the people in the first group made to driver safety by displaying the small sign greatly affected their decision about whether to accept the billboard. More than three-quarters of that group (76 percent) agreed to the billboard request; only 17 percent of the control group agreed.

The human need for consistency can be manipulated by marketers, who, as Cialdini explains, will go to great lengths to get consumers to commit to their product. It's called the "foot-in-the-door" technique. It applies to seemingly meaningless commitments such as requiring consumers to send in a card that describes how they use a product in order to enter a drawing for a cash prize. Hey, no purchase necessary.

We certainly don't advocate manipulating your schmoozing contacts. But you should understand the powerful way in which even a perceived investment in a bet, cause, brand – or relationship — can be. You may be rightly concerned about imposing on a contact and should keep that in the back of your mind. But you should also understand the strong drive for consistency that comes with commitment. If you keep in mind what the relationship means to the other person, rather than just what it means to you, you should be able to understand why a contact would be willing to continue helping you.

Fundraiser Juliet Gumbs gives a perfect example of how following up can pay off. While working as director of development for the nonprofit organization Poets and Writers, Gumbs developed a relationship with an independently wealthy woman from Wyoming. Eventually the woman agreed to endow a program with half a million dollars. After the woman gave the half million, Gumbs told the program directors that she felt that the woman would give more.

"They said, 'What? She just gave half a million dollars!'" Gumbs says. "They figured, you get your money, and then you go away, you don't bother them anymore.'"

Vault Profile: Juliet Gumbs

The daughter of a U.S. postal worker and a native of St. Thomas in the Virgin Islands, Juliet Gumbs has hobnobbed with the New York elite as a fundraiser for close to two decades. She didn't always find it so easy.

"Although I seem like an outgoing and engaging person, I had to learn that behavior," she says. "I dislike huge parties with lots of schmoozing, but I think of this as a challenge."

Schmoozing for dollars: Juliet Gumbs

The world of fundraising is notoriously dependent on personal contacts. "They always ask you who you know in the fundraising circle," she explains. "That's why it's so hard to move from Dallas to New York." After spending about 15 years as director of development at nonprofit and academic organizations, Gumbs decided to go into business for herself as a fundraising consultant. She counsels organizations on how to put together campaigns and is currently focusing on running workshops that concentrate on fundraising for minority, religious, and women's groups

Gumbs started her professional life as an anthropologist and a researcher. She grew up in the Lower East Side of Manhattan, where she says she was acutely aware of the cultural variety surrounding her. "You had Chinatown, Little Italy, you had the original New York Ghetto." After college, she did a stint with the American Red Cross in Korea and later traveled throughout Asia. Returning to the U.S., she had a job lined up studying populations in the Sea Islands off the coast of the Carolinas, who speak a distinctive dialect called Gullah.

Although she describes herself as exceedingly bookish in her earlier years, even Gumbs' early professional life has the fingerprints of schmoozing. The research position was found through a childhood friend. "She was taking a course in Columbia, and thought of me when she met this linguistic researcher. He called, introduced himself, we met in D.C., went out to lunch," Gumbs says. "I was in the Far East, and I received a packet with a prospectus about the project, and my name was already listed as a staff member."

Since her early start, Gumbs has gone right on schmoozing. After going into business for herself, she built up her database of contacts from 172 to 1,800 in four years. In the months preceding her meeting with a Vault editor, she had lined up a gig lecturing in New Orleans through a woman she met at a fundraising conference in Philadelphia and was also scheduled to travel to Oklahoma to give a series of workshops – a job found through a college friend who set her up with a woman he met at a Chamber of Commerce luncheon.

"The American myth is if you are smart and do your work, you will get there. Immigrants and people of color are fed this myth that if you're smart and do your work, you'll succeed," she says. Gumbs learned early on that hard work sometimes isn't enough. "My father used to say 'Contacts, contacts, contacts. It's all about contacts.'"

Gumbs decided that the woman would like to see the fruits of this investment. She sent the woman copies of books that writers who had been funded by her contribution had published. A short write-up about the woman, who dabbled in painting, was included in a brochure the organization sent out. The woman was invited to a reading in New York by one of the program's writers – she came and mingled with writers, some supported by Poets and Writers, some not. ("If you give half a million dollars, you can afford to come to New York for something like a reading," Gumbs notes wisely.)

"I made her feel a part of what she was giving to," Gumbs says. Since her initial gift, the woman has given tens of thousands of dollars more. When Gumbs left Poets and Writers, the woman was discussing a three-year commitment of giving, she says.

Keeping track of your circle

Okay, so you're not daunted by the prospect of keeping in touch with your numerous friends and acquaintances. Now – how are you going to do it? First and foremost, you have to make sure you can reach them. This may be simple if you stay in touch with only four or five people regularly, but becomes a problem somewhere in the double digits. What's a person to do with hundreds of contacts, or thousands?

There are tools that can be used to keep track of your contacts. There are computer databases, Rolodexes, digital organizers, address books, spreadsheets, personal calendars and brains. Each of these tools has its own advantages and disadvantages, but a schmoozer knows that just having them is not enough. Addresses and phone numbers change, people switch jobs, people get married and change their names.

With finesse, however, keeping track of people can be easy and fun. Since his junior year at Harvard, Internet entrepreneur Kaleil Isaza-Tuzman has been compiling a list of friends and relatives on an Excel spreadsheet. Isaza realized the necessity of keeping up-to-date information on friends' whereabouts after transferring to Harvard from Brown University. Tuzman spent his first year at Brown, then took a year off from school to surf in Hawaii. When he arrived at Harvard as a transfer student, Tuzman realized that he had lost touch with many of his friends from Brown.

"When I was getting close to finishing school (at Harvard), I thought that I needed to get information down so I could keep track of people," he says about starting his spreadsheet. Now, his list is seven pages long – Tuzman prints it out every few weeks, pops it in a pocket, and makes notes on it when he learns of a change in a friend's information. As for keeping track of his friends? Tuzman says he regularly calls college alumni offices to track down friends from Brown and Harvard University to get their latest info.

AIN'T NOBODY CAN'T BE FOUND

Want to track down a long-lost buddy or business associate? You may not go to the lengths of hiring a private investigator, but the pros can at least give you some tips. Mike McKeever has more than 20 years of experience as a P.I. To hear McKeever talk, it's not about punching out the bad guys or wearing funky masks. Instead the key, at least to the missing person part of the business, is to "just go with what seems logical to you." "The one thing I would say is try and see if the parent is in the old place, and 50 percent of the time that's true," McKeever tells us. "Start at the beginning. Maybe their parents are still there."

If you're really interested in tracking somebody down, resourcefulness and persistence will get you to your destination. McKeever tells one story of finding the biological mother of a client.

Ain't Nobody Can't Be Found, cont'd...

"I didn't even know her name," he says. "What I knew was that in 1967 her father owned a hardware store, and she was in the wallpaper business in Philadelphia. I was working from that."

"I thought to myself, I'm looking for the wallpaper historian of Philadelphia, the guy who knows everything about the wallpaper business in Philly," McKeever says. "I finally got a hold of that person after a bunch of phone calls. He told me, 'Oh you must be looking for so-and-so.'"

Although he then had the name of the woman, McKeever was concerned about a possible name change because of a marriage. So, he found the courthouse that handled the adoption. By checking court records, he found the name of the lawyer who handled the adoption. Although the lawyer did not want to talk about the case, McKeever found a willing ear in the attorney's secretary. "She was sympathetic, even though the lawyer was by the book," he recalls. "She told me, 'I heard that [the woman's] brother was in the wholesale liquor business in the Virgin Islands.'" McKeever made some calls to the Virgin Islands, but found that the woman's brother had retired to Virginia. "I called him, said 'I'm looking for your sister, it's a matter of a small inheritance. It's these two old ladies down the block who really liked her... He had her call me." When the woman called, McKeever verified her identity, and then smoothly backed out.

Schmoozing the multitudes

Organizing your contacts is crucial. Like Isaza, Jay Alix, whose Michigan-based firm, Jay Alix & Associates, is at the top of the corporate turnaround business (having helped restructure National Car Rental System, Unisys and Wang Laboratories), carries around printed lists of his contacts. His list is a bit longer than Isaza's – nearly 90 pages of teensy type, as described in a profile of Alix in *The Wall Street Journal*. He keeps in touch with hundreds of people with a system of notes and names written on 3-by-5 index cards that he buys by the tens of thousands. Many of Alix's major projects – such as the Wang Labs job, and a $4 million project with the discount drug chain Phar-Mor – have come from personal contacts.

Not only can keeping your contacts in a row get you to the top of an industry like the corporate turnaround business, it can also help you get to the top of the free world. In a series for *The Washington Post*, David Maraniss reported how Bill Clinton kept a cardboard box filled with alphabetized and note-filled index cards to keep track of contacts as a young, aspiring politician. Each card listed the names and phone numbers of classmates, professors, and other acquaintances. By 1980 the card file had more than 10,000 contacts and included information about conversations or meetings Clinton had with them along with dates of correspondence.

Following up

By 1982, Maraniss reported, Clinton's file had been computerized, and campaign workers pumped out thousands of letters, with different letters for categories such as first-time supporters, teachers, and the elderly. However, not all the letters were fund-raising solicitations. Clinton's office devoted equal energy to what his aides called a GTMY letter, or Glad-to-Meet-You letter, sent as follow-ups to meetings. Quick follow-up and continued contact, Clinton knows (as do all good schmoozers), are as important as the initial meeting.

Widespread follow-up is key in the fashion world as well. As the manager of the men's department at a top fashion boutique in New York, Jennifer doesn't take any new clients. She leaves that to her staff. Instead, armed with a client book with hundreds of names, she taps into her already sizable base of clients.

For Jennifer, staying in touch starts almost immediately. The first thing she does is call a client about a purchase shortly after it has been delivered. "They'll remember these things," she says. "When you pay $2,000 for a suit, you expect personal service."

When it comes to meeting mentors or other contacts while looking for a job, this means following up shortly after a meeting (within a couple of days) with a thank-you note or a quick call of thanks. The early follow-up serves two purposes. One, it shows you not to be an ingrate. Two, it reinforces the meeting in your contact's mind.

A Simple Thanks is All We Ask

Small social niceties are appreciated well out of proportion to the actual time it takes to do them. A thank-you note both recognizes that something nice has been done for you and fixes you in the recipient's mind as a kind, thoughtful person. Indeed, even the successful and busy who take the time out to be socially gracious are recognized as such. President George Bush and his wife Barbara were famous in Washington for their rafts of thank-you notes. Today, people remember Bush as a man of high character (at least when compared to his successor). Coincidence? Perhaps not.

Quality counts too — in one celebrated study, a researcher who sent out poor-quality cards to people he didn't know received a response rate of 10 percent — but when he sent out glossy, attractive cards, his hit rate went up to 37 percent. Given this evidence, you may want to take the time out to have personalized thank-you cards made up. Don't worry: not all personal engravers charge Tiffany rates. Shop around.

Send a thank-you note whenever someone's done you a favor. Send them when you get a present, send them when you attend dinner at someone's house, send them to the person who organizes your going-away party at the office, send them to the professor who writes you a recommendation for law school. Don't procrastinate — keep a box next to your phone or on your desk. Make a note whenever someone does something worthy of a thank-you note — and send it right away. Your action may be one of the first steps towards a schmoozy, civil society.

TOOLS OF THE SCHMOOZER

We, as a species, have managed to rise above others largely because of one idiosyncrasy: our love of tools. Whether it's been the spear or the printing press, we've turned to gadgets to find a solution. And so in the battle to ensure that no number's left undialed, humanity has continued its habit of fiddling with technology to find a solution.

The Rolodex, the first major contact management tool of the Information Age, was created by New York entrepreneur Arnold Neustadter in 1948, as merely another product in his offbeat "odex" office supply line. At the time the odex product list also included such long-forgotten creations as the Clipodex, a note pad that attached itself to a secretary's knee, and the Swivodex, a non-spill inkwell that had the misfortune of being introduced at the beginning of the ballpoint pen revolution. The Rolodex, however, transformed Neustadter's company from a small-time operation to the home of a national icon.

Over the next 40 years the Rolodex became indispensable to the truly connected. It wasn't until the business a-go-go 1980s that the clunky Rolodex lost its position as the schmooze toy of choice for mobile businesspeople. Carrying a Rolodex around all day was only slightly more practical that carrying your secretary on your shoulders.

Enter the Filofax, a tasteful leatherbound business organizer that looks like a book. For the first 60 years of its existence the London-based Filofax company, founded in 1921, had been content selling its organizational supplies to British clergymen and army officials. But after the company was bought by husband and wife yuppie-visionaries David and Lesley Collischon, Filofax, hyped as a chic, essential organizational item, arrived at counters of stationery stores and retail outlets. The move was timed perfectly: the rise in transportation efficiency, combined with the Thatcher-Reagan status-crazed consumer boom, caused sales to skyrocket. Handheld, sleek and sexy, the Filofax offered networkers a chance to gather the information that usually sat in a heap on their desks into a manageable and portable status symbol.

The new millennium has demanded even more efficient methods of organizing. As computers continue to take larger roles in our lives, many have dreamed of a utopian product that would do to the paper-based organizer what the Xerox machine did to carbon paper. And after years of false prophets in the form of numerous half-assed pocket organizers, a new generation of organizers has been born in the form of the PalmPilot, the handheld computer that puts a Motorola chip to work for your schmoozing needs.

Unlike earlier electronic incarnations, the PalmPilot enables users to download information directly from their desktops and quickly synchronize information on both screens. The

Tools of the Schmooze, cont'd...

versatile PalmPilot can also work as a pager, remote control, alarm clock, notepad, game system, and expense log. The little bugger even offers e-mail retrieval and Web browsing options.

The accessible code attracts programming enthusiasts, who spend their spare time taking the Pilot's already expansive capabilities even further. The latest PalmPilots store thousands of addresses, appointments, memos and to-do items, and hundreds of e-mail messages – more computerized info than NASA had aboard its first satellite. And all you need is to remember where you have to be next Tuesday.

After that initial follow-up, Jennifer continues to keep in touch with clients, no matter how small a purchase they may have made. "I have all my sales staff writing follow-up letters," she says. "And we contact them on the phone and in writing to tell them what's new in the collection." Following up is not all sales-oriented, either, in the upper echelons of the fashion industry. "We send cards for Christmas," Jennifer says. "Sometimes also for birthdays and anniversaries."

Jennifer takes her time when corresponding with clients (see sidebar on p. 172). "I handwrite them," she says. "Nowadays others use computers. But I feel handwriting gives an important personal touch."

Vault Profile: J.D. Crouch

"I tried paper organizers, but they were so thick that they didn't fit my lifestyle," explains J.D. Crouch II, who with partner Kenny West turned an enthusiasm for the PalmPilot personal organizer into a multi-million dollar business in less than a year. "What I really liked was the idea that something could fit in your pocket ... I was looking for something like a PalmPilot for a long time."

He has the whole world in his Palm

Crouch, an advisor during high-level disarmament talks with the former Soviet Union during the Reagan administration, senior Pentagon official in the first Bush Administration, and now a professor of international politics at Southwestern Missouri State University, is also co-founder of PalmPilot Gear H.Q. The Arlington, Texas-based company sells software for the popular PalmPilot organizer, manufactured by 3Com. Crouch's company allows enthusiasts to buy everything from titanium covers for their organizers to software that enables users to look up street maps and identify their longitude and latitude coordinates.

Crouch, 40, says he bought his first electronic organizers in the early 1980s, ones made by Casio and Radio Shack. "Both my partner [West] and I were first-adopters," explaining that "these are the people who, when something new comes out, they go out and buy it, it doesn't matter how much it costs. If the product sells for $399 and they can get it [now] or they can get it for $359 a month later, they want it now."

Crouch's professed love of techno-gadgets aside, the professor believes that a small contact organizer is increasingly essential for the New Business Order. "I was more interested in it from an academic perspective of how networking and global networking would affect commerce."

"There were a couple of things that made the PalmPilot attractive," he says. "I was away from the office quite a bit, away from the computer. For someone who is moving around, traveling, having an organizer that you can access all of your contact data from is very important."

Not only is contact management facing new challenges because of increasing mobility, Crouch says, but also because of the rise of hyphenates like his own professor-business owner-disarmament-advisor self. "People have many different aspects to their lives these days. The notion of 'I'm a sheet metal worker and that's all I do' is increasingly diminishing," he says. "There's an increasing number of people who either have to take two different jobs or who are interested in doing a variety of things in their lives ... and these organizers are very useful for that."

The idea of PalmPilot Gear was conceived in summer 1997. It was hatched that same summer and passed into adulthood almost immediately. In its first year of operations, PalmPilot Gear did millions of dollars in business.

"Our initial thinking was that we were going to do this, we might be able to pull a couple hundred dollars a month out of it ... It was wild, it just hit at the right time," Crouch says.

The evolution of contact management

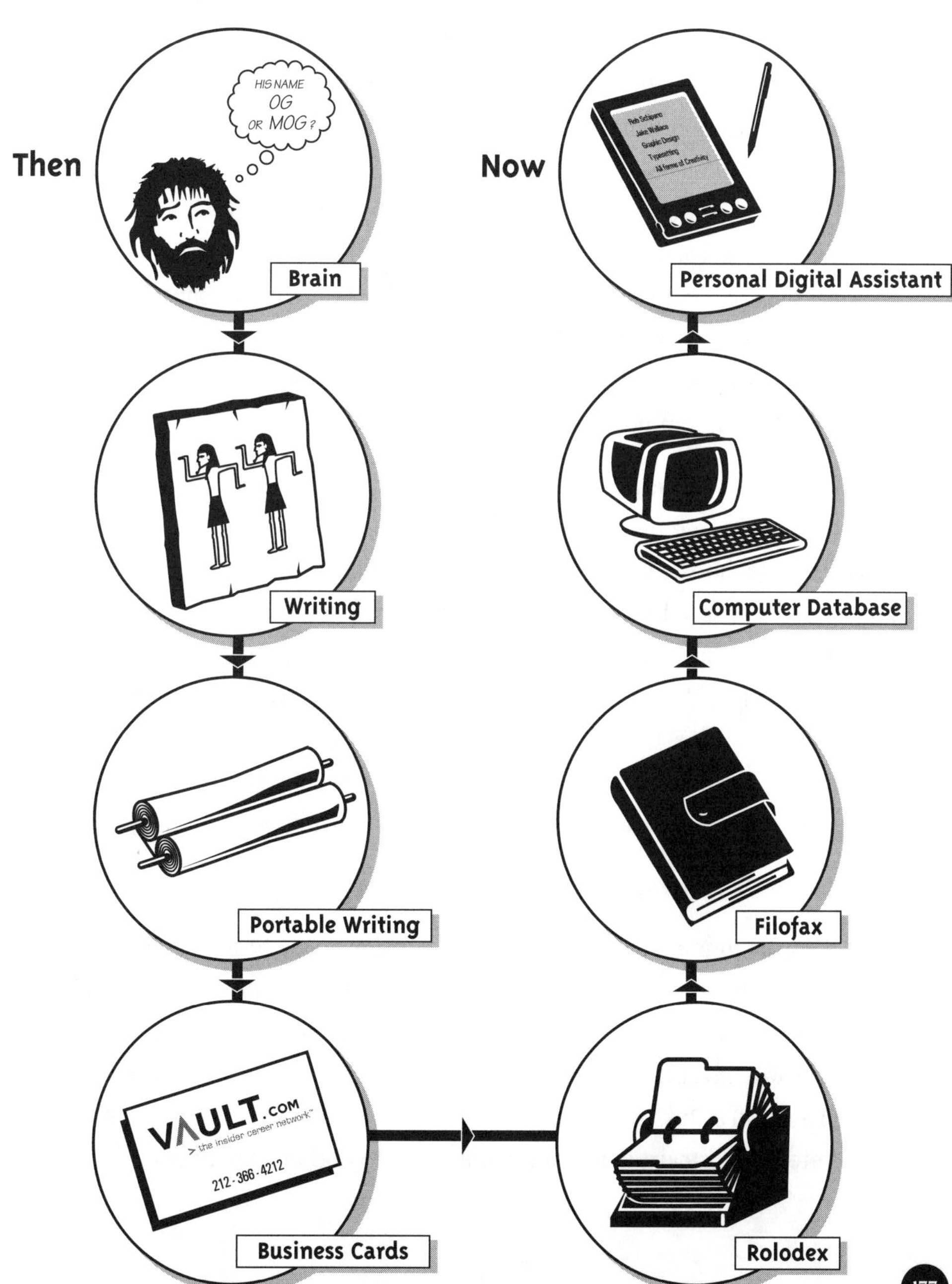

Use your post office

Mass mailings, like the one Jennifer sends to her clients, are one way to stay in touch with your friends and acquaintances. They may seem impersonal and worklike, but they need not be. Holiday cards are the most common mass mailing, and we encourage you to send these cards if you enjoy doing it, but keep in mind that those to whom you are sending the cards are being deluged by other cards. Your card gets lost among those other cards, not to mention among stress about presents, parties, and relatives. Some people mail cards on alternative holidays to set themselves apart. Chris Shays, a congressman from Connecticut, sends out Valentine's Day cards to his supporters.

Other mass mailings work too. When Russ Korins, 25, decided after one year of Georgetown Law School to put his legal education on hold to work at a hot New York information technology company, he decided to use a simulated press release to announce the bold move to the Big Apple. "First, I wanted to tell my friends that I was back in New York," Korins says, "but more importantly, I wanted to avoid having the same conversation a thousand times: Why did you leave Georgetown and when are you going back? What are you doing in New York?" Korins sent out a faux newsletter announcing his move (see next page).

Fun for Russ, funny for us, and very effective.

If you're running your own business, it makes sense to send mailings out giving updates about major events. These don't need to be chest-thumping exercises — you shouldn't send out leaflets that say "JOE's GARAGE CELEBRATES THOUSANDTH CUSTOMER." But when you have a change like Russ's relocation — say you're opening a new office — a letter or postcard is in good taste. Other good opportunities for mass mailings: a job change, a promotion that changes your phone number, even a new pet. *Someone* wants to see pictures of your pet ferret.

FOR IMMEDIATE RELEASE

D.C. Follies Continue

Washington loses another one; Barry confused

Washington, D.C., July 20 -- Ross Korins will escape from the District of Columbia on Monday, July 28, when he moves back to New York. He will live at home for a short time until he moves onto his all-time favorite island, Manhattan. He is starting a job in New York on August 4. He is taking a year off from law school and plans to return to school in fall 1998.

In a statement earlier this week, District Mayor Marion Barry expressed surprise that anyone would want to move out of the District. "We recently bought a new snowplow, doubling the size of our fleet," Barry said.

Barry added, "In D.C., you can get a fresh deli sandwich custom-made in under 25 minutes. And some pizza places are open on weekends as late as 10:00 p.m. As I always say, Washington is a good city, getting better."

Juliet Gumbs sends postcards informing her contacts about workshops she is giving or radio appearances. The postcard, she says, is also a good way to keep track of people. If the card comes back, "it gives me an excuse to call, to find out who the replacement at that position is."

You may wish simply to do a quarterly update letter to all your friends and acquaintances, but if you do this, write personalized comments in the margin or at the end of the letter. This allows you both to put more information into each communication and make people feel like you are saying something to them personally.

Aside from mass mailings, there are other, more personal ways to keep up with people through the mail if you don't have the time to meet for lunch. Part of what makes snail mail appealing to schmoozers is that it has the feel of being very personal, but at the same time does not require massive calendar checking and endless games of phone tag.

When Kaleil Isaza Tuzman, our Internet entrepreneur, reads a newspaper or magazine article that reminds him of someone, he'll send it to the person with a little note. The key to making such a technique successful, he says, is not to dawdle. When you see an article or postcard that makes you think of a person, he says, clip it out and send it right away. Tuzman also says that "whenever I'm travelling, I always try to send a bunch of postcards to people I may not have seen for a while." Postcards, we think, are a terrific way to drop someone a note. They're short, they're fun, and people tend to hang onto them — if nothing else, to decorate their refrigerators.

Vault Profile: Kaleil Isaza-Tuzman

Kaleil Isaza-Tuzman, 29, is the co-founder of govworks (now called govOneSolutions), a site that brings government services to citizens and businesses over the Web. A native of Colombia and a graduate of Harvard University, Isaza-Tuzman estimates that every week, he calls or otherwise gets in touch with (through e-mail, letters, etc.) at least three people he hasn't contacted in six months. You can do the math and figure out how many people Isaza-Tuzman keeps in his schmoozing circle.

The Accidental Schmoozer

Isaza-Tuzman grew up in Medellin, Colombia —his father, a government official and adjunct professor at Smith College in the U.S., is Colombian; his mother is a native of Israel. "I spent a lot of time bumping from one place to another," he says, explaining that he spent summers in the U.S. and Israel as a kid. "I kind of got used to fitting in." He moved to the U.S. for high school, but his jumping around didn't stop. "Through high school, I switched schools five, six times," he recounts. After high school and during college, Isaza-Tuzman took time off to live in Mexico City, Hawaii, and Mumbai, India. Isaza-Tuzman is grateful for his itinerant and varied upbringing. "I was kind of taught to be interested in different experiences," he says.

With so many people to keep in touch with, Isaza-Tuzman's motivation for staying with his friends and acquaintances is simple. "I'm a pleasure seeker," he says. "I enjoy keeping in touch with people, so it's easy for me."

Get in touch with tech

And for the techno-literate, there's always e-mail forwarding. "If I see an article that strikes me, I'll drop them a line, or shoot them an e-mail — it's a little more efficient," Erik Jorgensen, a product manager at Microsoft (see profile on p. 208) says. "I'll also send and receive e-mails of job opportunities. if we have something that I think would be well-suited for someone, I'll send that along."

We'll talk more about using technology to schmooze in a later chapter, but for now consider what George Bell, former chairman and CEO of Excite@Home tells Vault: "Most of the people I used to call my friends don't call me that anymore. They don't bother to call me. I rarely get in touch with people. But e-mail has helped — it has made communication much more efficient. I can go home and deal with 20 to 30 e-mails at the end of the day. About once a week I'll get an e-mail from a friend of mine who I haven't spoken to in a while. I try to respond to all the e-mail I get."

Finally, there's always reaching out and touching someone over the phone. Isaza-Tuzman calls people whenever he thinks of them, even if he knows he will just get their voice mail. He does this about twice a day. Jim, our Connecticut school board head, says he stays in touch with some of his supporters by phone, especially one of them, who has recently fallen ill. "Occasionally I just pick up the phone and call her. It's not so much a technique as doing the right thing — it's the least I can do. It's just the way that I am. Is that a technique? I guess it is, but it's also who I am."

The middleman: the ultimate in schmoozing

One of the best ways to keep in touch with contacts is to introduce people to each other. This is perhaps the highest form of schmoozing. This is not to say that it is in any way esoteric or difficult or rare. It is a high form of schmoozing because it pulls many of the techniques discussed in previous chapters together into one powerful punch.

Say you know that an acquaintance, Stacy, wants to get into the publishing industry. You happen to know Carlos, who used to work for a major publishing house. You give Carlos' number to Stacy and call him in advance to tell him to expect a call from her. You are doing several things here: You are helping Stacy, you are flattering Carlos, and you are keeping in touch with both of them. In a week or so, you can call both of them to find out whether their talk or meeting was helpful.

Once you start acting as the middle link in such chains, the chain of referrals becomes never-ending. This happens in part because there is a perception of a favor being performed, even if all that is really happening is everybody is helping everybody out and feeling good about it. It seems as if Carlos is doing you a favor by trying to help Stacy, but really, he's just meeting another person, whose acquaintance, you probably expect (if you have confidence in her), will bring him enjoyment and possibly, future help.

Part of playing the middleman is being a conveyor and distributor of hellos and regards. If someone says, "Oh, you're going to see Carlos? Tell him 'hi,' you should try to remember to do it. For many people, the request to "Say 'hi' for me" has all the imperative strength of the exhortation to "Have a nice day." But passing on regards is valuable, if nothing else, as fodder for conversation: "Oh, Carlos says 'hi'? What's he up to?" Since time immemorial – or at least since humans began moving around enough to meet people that they didn't have daily contact with – talking through people has been an important part of communication. Whole hours of conversations can be had based on the "What's she up to now?" theme. "Whenever I see someone, I may say, 'Have you seen so-and-so?'" Internet entrepreneur Isaza-Tuzman says. "If they stay in touch, I say to send my regards."

When it comes to staying in touch with business associates, and exploring potential job opportunities, Erik Jorgensen of Microsoft says keeping in touch with headhunters is an "indirect" way to keep in touch with others in the same industry. "Every time I get a call from a new headhunter whom I don't know, they'll say 'Hey, so-and-so gave me your name.'" Jorgensen says he'll occasionally pick the brains of headhunters to find out what the referrer's up to.

The use of a conversation chain instead of a telephone wire or postal service works both ways, of course. "They always ask if they can use your name," Jorgensen says about the referrals he gives to headhunters. "And inevitably I say yes."

KEY CONCEPTS

- Understand the tendency toward consistency — don't be afraid of recontacting someone.
- Follow up immediately with someone who helps you with a thank-you note.
- Use mass mailings, e-mail, phone calls (even messages on voice mail), postcards, and forwarded articles to stay in touch.
- Keep your information on friends and acquaintances organized and up-to-date.

Vernon Jordan

Walking with Vernon Jordan, the premier Washington powerbroker, on the streets of D.C. is an experience full of interruptions.

"We were probably stopped six times," a senior Treasury official, who had this very experience, told *The Washington Post*. "They were people with varying degrees of familiarity with Vernon. We ran into a secretary and he asked her about her son, by name, and he ticked off three facts about him. Each person he told as he left them, 'If you need anything done, don't hesitate to call me.'"

Mr. Jordan wants to do you a favor

This ability of Jordan to befriend many types of people and to show that he cares about them has fueled his rise from a pioneer in the civil rights movement to his current perch as one of the most powerful men in Washington. His connections in the establishment – in business (including universities and foundations, he serves as a director on 15 boards), in politics (he is Bill Clinton's golfing buddy), and in the media (he is close friends with the journalistic elite) – are extraordinary. This makes him extremely valuable in Washington as someone who can get things done. For instance, when Clinton wanted to gauge Colin Powell's interest in becoming part of his Cabinet, he asked Jordan to broach the sensitive subject.

Jordan offers his services not only to the rich and powerful but also to the young and unconnected, realizing that they may someday gain prominence. (Jordan befriended Clinton in the early '70s, when the future President was

Jordan profile, cont'd...

fresh out of law school). No wonder *The Economist* calls Jordan "a grand Washington schmoozer."

"He was not an official member of the president's staff or the Cabinet, but there is such a thing as a kitchen cabinet dating back to the days of Andrew Jackson," Clinton's former spokesman, Mike McCurry, has said. "If there is such a thing, Vernon is in it."

Finally, Jordan realizes the advantages of subtlety when getting his message across. He never explicitly tells others just how much he has helped a person, but he makes sure that his efforts are not forgotten. Remember that senior Treasury official who took a stroll with Jordan? He has a feeling that Jordan is the reason why he has his current plum job.

"I think Vernon put in a good word for me," the official said. "He's never, ever said that. After I got the job, I'd bump into him and he'd just say, 'Tell [former Treasury Secretary] Bob Rubin I said hi.'"

CHAPTER 9

SCHMOOZING TO FIND A JOB

Look ma, no classifieds

"I tell my clients that 15 percent of jobs are filled through the newspaper, five percent are filled through companies like mine, and 80 percent are filled through word-of-mouth," says Beth Anrig, the owner of Beth Anrig and Associates, a job placement service in Connecticut. Anrig places individuals in positions in a wide variety of industries, ranging from banking to publishing. "Do you know how most jobs are filled?" Anrig asks. "A manager asks a couple of people if they know anyone good."

We've moved past the point where we expect that jobs will be mainly filled through company recruiting and advertising. According to widely-cited statistics, 75 to 80 percent of all job seekers find their new position through referrals; most openings never see the light of day (or newsprint). By schmoozing, you make word-of-mouth work in your favor. You can learn about a variety of industries and make friends and contacts whom you can call upon for career advice or assistance. Now how to do it?

The Basics

Put the word out

Before Tamara Totah found her present position as a headhunter with the search firm The Oxbridge Group, she investigated career options in a variety of fields, the music industry among them. "I told everyone until it was coming out of their ears," she says. Her first meeting was with a friend of a friend who did marketing at Warner Music. Next she met with a contact who worked at a radio station. Soon she was going to music parties.

"It just kept going and going," Totah says. This classic schmoozing effort doesn't have the usual happy ending of the heroine finding a job, but to hear Totah talk about it, investigating the music world was far from a waste. She says she stopped pursuing the field, because "I realized that the music industry was vile. But for a while, I was going to every concert that came into town."

When you're schmoozing for a job, the first step is to bring up the fact that you're looking. Ron Nelson, a career transition counselor in Connecticut, says, "You can mention it to the guy you buy the newspaper from, or someone you always see when you're pumping gas. As long as they know your name and to say hi to you, they become someone you should talk to. You should talk to everyone. You should talk to people even when you have no idea why you are talking to them. This is a very small world, and everyone knows someone." The easiest way to get to the subject is simply to ask people what they do for a living. After telling you, they are likely to inquire, "And what do you do?" That's your opportunity to talk about your job search.

The same is true when it comes to bringing up the subject with friends and acquaintances. "First, ask them what they're up to career-wise," Anrig advises. "They'll tell you, and then ask, 'How about you?' Then you can talk about what you want." But if you ever feel uncomfortable about talking about your career plans while schmoozing, don't. Schmoozing should never make you, or anyone else, uncomfortable. If you keep in touch with the people you schmooze (and you should!) the right opportunity will arise soon enough.

At the same time, if you're comfortable with it, don't be afraid of repeating yourself. Anrig admits you might feel like a broken record, "but people might need to hear your story once or twice before they start thinking about how they can help you."

If you keep in touch with people, and let them know you're looking, they're bound to remember you when they hear of something. Erik Jorgensen, a product manager at Microsoft who has helped bring four friends to the software giant, keeps a "mental rolodex of the folks I know, and what I think their strengths are. When I hear of something, or if I'm asked if I know of anyone, I'll let the appropriate people know." For example, says Jorgensen, "I knew a guy who loved game software. When I was asked if I knew of anyone for a game position, he was the first person who came to mind."

What are you looking for?

Of course it helps to know what kind of job you're looking for. But if you don't, just reconfigure your mission – find out about as many different kind of jobs as you can. Say something along the lines of "I'm thinking of leaving the teaching profession, and I'm exploring possible career changes. Can you tell me a bit more about what you do as a pet groomer?"

Don't be overly direct. It's much better to say something along the lines of "Well, I'm hoping to transition from law into publishing," or "My previous accounting company downsized, and I'm looking for another position in the profession," than "I'm looking for a job." The latter sounds harsher and more desperate, and if the person you're chatting with happens to work in that profession, they may feel put on the spot.

Schmoozing to find a job when in school

If you're still in school, you have golden schmoozing opportunities all around you. Many students forget that there are numerous people at their university who already know them and are predisposed to want them to succeed – their professors. If you think your history professor only knows about the French Revolution, think again. He's probably pretty savvy about life in this century as well.

Make sure you are on a first-name basis with each and every one of your professors. Even if you're enrolled in huge lecture classes and can barely see the prof, figure out when his or her office hours are (hint: they'll be printed on the syllabus or posted on the office door) and go. Most professors only see students when they're begging for extensions on papers or explaining how they slept through the midterm. Your schmoozing should come as a welcome change.

Introduce yourself to your professor at the beginning of the semester. Tell them you're looking forward to taking the class, and if you're majoring (or thinking about it) in the subject, let them know that too. If you have any questions about something in lecture or are curious about something you've read, ask. But make sure to ask non-class-related questions as well. How did they get interested in sociology? What research are they doing now? Can they recommend any other good classes?

Because, after all, you ultimately want to get a job after you graduate, ask your professor for advice about that too. What have other students in his/her subject done after graduation? What does the professor recommend you do? You'd be surprised how many professors consult with companies part-time. If you're at a larger university, you might want to consider taking a class at your university's business or law school, as professors at professional schools often have an even wider variety of career contacts.

Tap alumni resources

Other woefully underused routes to schmoozing for a job in school are career counselors and alumni.

Career counselors want to help you get a job. That's *their* job. At the same time, they also have to find jobs for the other couple of thousand students at your university. But you, smart schmoozer that you are, have an advantage – not all those students are going to bother to schmooze their career counselors. As early as possible in your school career, go to your school career center, introduce yourself and discuss your career goals. Thank your counselor for any particularly good advice or leads he gives you. Most students neglect career counselors until the spring of their senior year. Don't make the same mistake.

Alumni already have a point of similarity with you. Ron Nelson points out, "Just having that little thing like a school connection takes you from 'Who the hell are you and why are you calling me?' to 'Oh, okay, you went to Vanderbilt too, what can I do for you?' It's not a big thing, but it's enough."

Tamara Totah, the former headhunter for The Oxbridge Group, also recommends using alumni contacts from your school, although she cautions that you should never directly ask them for a job. "The minute they hear that they get worried," she says. "Talk to them about what different opportunities may be available in the industry. People will spend 30 minutes with you. They know how tough it is."

Always intern

Internships are an essential component of the job hunting process. Part of the reason they are so valuable is that they give you work experience that later can be used to help you in a job search.

Once you get inside a company as an intern, you should not feel restrained by the department that you're working in – or even by your assigned supervisor. Figure out what you most want to do in the organization and schmooze the person who does it. A good way to do this is to ask this person to lunch. A good line is: "I'm trying to absorb as much information as I can in this internship, and what you do seems particularly interesting. I wonder if you are available for lunch anytime this week."

The person will almost always say "Yes." When he describes what he does at lunch, try to relate the skills that he employs to skills that you have. For example, if he tells you about the press release he is writing for company X, slip in how that's similar to your college newspaper writing experience. With any luck, your schmoozee will then offer you a chance to draft a press release. If not, try to give him another gentle nudge: "Oh, writing press releases seems like so much fun!"

When you are given menial errands to do, take it in good cheer. No one likes a whiner. If you feel like you must say something, couch it in humor. One State Department intern remembers telling his boss, "Although being a Deputy Assistant Secretary of Photocopying has its moments, I was wondering if I could do more substantive work here?" The question got his message across without rancor – and the intern received some interesting assignments. Remember: as long as you do a few things that look impressive, you won't have to put on your resume that you ran errands and photocopied stuff 99 percent of the time. So instead of complaining about your menial tasks – or even non-verbally grumbling by acting dour – express an interest in doing specific, substantive work.

Vault Profile: Price Hicks

A winner of four Emmys for her work in public television and now Director of Educational Programs and Services for the Academy of Television Arts & Sciences in Los Angeles (the people who award the Emmys), Price Hicks was a late starter. "I had an internship when I was 41," she says. "I snuck in when no one was looking."

Priceless Price

Hicks says she received an art degree in college "but never used it." After raising a family, Price went back to school and designed her own communications master's degree program, eventually discovering the radio/TV/film department. As the program wound down, Hicks went looking for information on internships, hoping to learn more about the industry she was studying. She was met with surprise. "No one had ever asked for an internship before," she says. Armed with a letter of recommendation, Hicks made the rounds to all the studios in search of an opportunity but was told at place after place: "You can only observe, you can't write anything." But after a fortuitous trip to the local public TV station, Hicks landed an internship with promise. "I was taken on as a 20-hour unpaid intern," Hicks recalls. "Before my internship was over, they offered me a job. A year and a half later I was a producer."

The time was right for a talented producer in public TV, as PBS was just coming into its own with the introduction of shows such as *Sesame Street*. Hicks

Hicks profile, cont'd...

eventually inherited a couple of series. One, *Citywatchers,* a show about L.A., became her show – it won four Emmys.

Hicks left public television in 1982 and freelanced for a few years. She joined the Academy after a chance meeting at her old public station. At an event there, she ran into her former boss, James Loper, who had by then gone on to become Executive Director of the Academy of Television Arts & Sciences. "He asked what I was doing," Hicks recalls. "I said I really didn't know. He told me that they were going to establish an education department." After her interview, "They basically said I had the job. I met with them and we were off and running."

SCHMOOZING FROM THE MAIL ROOM UP

As part of her position with the Academy, Hicks oversees the organization's internship program. At the time of her arrival, the Academy had an internship program and an affiliated awards program, but they hadn't been fully developed. During Hicks' tenure, the Academy has added a mentorship program within the awards program, as well as an internship alumni newsletter.

Hicks has seen the popularity of internships in the television industry grow from the rare into the expected. "I'm amazed at how corporate America has embraced internships," Hicks says. "Today they are essential. You must have familiarity with the workplace."

"An internship is a contact," Hicks notes. "I don't know how anyone gets in without super contacts." Of course, Hicks makes sure to point out the 'necessary but not sufficient' rule of contacts: "Contacts don't help you unless you have something to bring to the table." The television industry requires work experience, and specifically, experience in the industry's capital city: "You need to move to L.A. and get along at a high-pressure time of the year. It's making a commitment to learning how to live in Los Angeles."

Of the Academy internship program, Hicks says, "We are not in the business of announcing star turns, we're in the business of building careers. Our internships are career builders." But Hicks warns interns that "you don't go right from the mail room to being Steven Spielberg." Success stories from the program have included the likes of Brannon Braga, a former *Star Trek* writer, now a producer. Within the program, each intern is mentored by a former intern, and interns often help each other. "I've never known one intern not to help another," Hick says. The organization tries to stay in touch with former interns. "The door is always open for them," she says. The Academy publishes a newsletter and an address list. Occasionally, Hicks gets calls from former interns looking for career advice. "We answer every phone call."

But perhaps more important than the experience you get as an intern are the people you meet. Make it your personal assignment to meet as many people as possible at the place you intern, as well as anyone who works with the people there. Keep in touch with your co-workers, supervisors and fellow interns after you leave your internship. Ensure they are up-to-date on your educational and career progress. You can do this through the methods discussed before – send holiday cards, call once in a while to see how things are doing at the "old homestead," and if you're in town, stop by the office or meet for lunch. That way, when a job opening appears, you'll be sure to hear about it.

But what if you do an internship and, after a few days or weeks, decide that public relations or pet grooming just isn't for you? Should you then give up, slack off, and forget about it? Should you not bother keeping in touch with the people you met at your internship? No, no, no! We shouldn't have to tell you that, even if you've suddenly decided you want to be an astronaut, the people at your internship may know someone who works at Kennedy Space Center. Or, unbeknownst to you, that woman at the next desk is the niece of Buzz Aldrin. But even if nothing and no one at your job connects to your current career passion right now, the people there should remember you as a cheerful, hardworking, friendly person – so when they do meet someone who's the human resources manager for NASA, they can tell you about it the next time you call.

Schmoozing for a job out of school

Once you're out of school, you'll have lost (sniff!) some of the support structure for which all your tuition dollars paid. What happens when you've found a job, and then found that you're not too happy with it? Don't be afraid – most people in this age of downsizing and corporate restructuring and increasing specialization change careers at least six times during their lives. With all the job hopping, people increasingly accept that job changing is a part of life. Your schmoozing talents will help you ease these transitions.

The informational interview

It's not a job interview – exactly. But it does get you face-to-face with someone in an industry that interests you. Informational interviews are an invaluable opportunity to learn about the inside scoop into the career field that interests you. Many people are prepared to spend 10 minutes to an hour of their time to talk to those looking for a job, assess their skills and background, and give them some pointers in breaking into their chosen field.

Says Beth Anrig, "I tell all my clients that the best thing to do is to set up informational interviews." One caveat – "never call them that," she says. Informational interviews sound too much like interviews, and that sounds like asking for a job. Everyone is over-networked, in the official sense. No one has the time anymore to do something that is just like a job.

So don't frame the "informational interview" as any kind of interview. Instead, say that you want to talk with them, or get coffee, or chat. Your goal is to have a conversation, not an interview. Ask semipersonal questions: What got you started in this industry? What other careers did you consider? Are you happy in your choice? At the same time, talk honestly and openly about your own career aspirations, and why the industry in question appeals to you. If you click, keep the person abreast of your career progress and decisions.

But never, says Totah, our erstwhile New York headhunter, ask for a job outright. "If they don't have one and you ask that, they're going to want to boot you out five minutes later." Totah says. "Believe me, if you're talking about careers, they know you want a job. If they like you and they can help you in some way they will." Schmoozing means you don't spell it out.

When calling someone for an informational interview, make it clear you are not asking for a job. The point is, if they like you, they will help you find a job. Appeal to your contact's expertise. "Everyone likes to give advice," says Anrig. "If you tell them that you are calling because a mutual acquaintance has suggested they are a real authority in their field or an inspiring example, they will be hard-pressed to turn you down."

Though the informational interview isn't a job interview (exactly), it's still important to do your research on the company and the industry. It's rude to waste someone's time during the workday, and it doesn't reflect well on you. "Most people are very generous about helping people make connections," says Wicke Chambers, our communications consultant from Atlanta. "I have a lot of business contacts and am willing to call up and set up informational interviews for people coming out of college and recent grads. I myself am approached for interviews constantly."

Vault Profile: Lara Rosenthal

New York writer and producer Lara Rosenthal, who has written for The Wall Street Journal, *the* Asian Wall Street Journal, *and* The Wall Street Journal Interactive Edition, *served as a freelance streaming video producer for Yahoo! and had full-time stints with CNN and Dow Jones, tells Vault how she schmoozes her way to jobs.*

Sweet smile; savvy schmoozer

I've never gone through college recruiting, used want ads, or done a mass mailing of resumes. I've always found my jobs though contacts. That's for a number of reasons. When you first graduate from college, the jobs available are so cookie-cutter. You're a consultant. You're an accountant. I felt like being pigeonholed wouldn't be good for me, and I still feel that way. The fact is that a lot of jobs available right now — most jobs, in fact – are not in those cookie-cutter categories. For example, the last job I had was working for Dow Jones on a TV show that airs in China, doing something like that requires an unusual set of skills – business knowledge, knowledge of Chinese culture, and Chinese language. You won't find a job like that through the want ads. You find jobs like that through meeting people and staying in touch with people who share your interests.

How did I get started? In 1991, when I graduated from college, I decided to go live in Asia. I was interested in getting some international experience, so I went on a program and enrolled in a university in Taiwan. I got my visa and living arrangements that way. Before that time I had studied biology and

Rosenthal profile, cont'd...

economics. The thing is, Taiwan is a very polluted place. After a while, my Chinese had improved and I had both foreign and Taiwanese friends. I decided I wanted to do something about the environmental situation in Taiwan, so I would go to parties and tell everyone that I wanted to do environmental consulting. Most people would just say, "Wow, that's a good idea." But one day I was talking to a group of people about careers, and this guy gave me the name of another guy, Greg.

I got Greg's work number and called his office. The man who answered the phone said, "Who's this?" and "What's the message?" I said, "This is Lara, and I wanted to know if Greg wants to go for Peking Duck tonight." The guy who answered the phone said, "OK, Greg will have dinner with you tonight. "How do you know?" I asked. "Because I'm his boss," he said.

That night I had dinner with both of them and spoke to them about what they were doing. It turned out the firm was doing exactly what I wanted to be doing. They asked me if I wanted to work on a project. Of course, I agreed. This small operation turned out to be the one consulting company in the country at that time that was doing this kind of work.

I came back to the U.S. and joined a gym. One day I was in aerobics and this woman I knew walked by. I'd known her briefly – before going to Taiwan, I had worked at CNN and she'd worked there too. I literally ran out of the class and said hi to her. I had just gotten back to the city and had lost touch with many old friends so I was thrilled to see someone I knew. She asked me what I was doing and I told her that I had just gotten back from Asia and was looking for a job. She gave me a number to call at Dow Jones, and I interviewed for the job in the television department and got it.

The point is that, I have always gravitated towards people with international experience. Any kind of career advancement is a side effect. I sometimes go to Asia Society events in New York, and I am on the China Roundtable, but it's because I'm interested in it. Maybe someday it will lead to something, or maybe not, but your interest has to be sincere – you can't look at people just in terms of what they can do for you.

However, Chambers says, "What I do mind is people asking to talk to me about my job and then having absolutely no idea what they want. I've interviewed with people who don't know whether they want to be a florist, an airline pilot or a public relations executive. I don't care a hill of beans if someone hasn't at least got an idea about what they want to do and how I can help."

Get inside the company

Even if you're switching jobs or industries and have been in the workforce for some time, it's not too late to do a sort of internship. Because your goal is to meet as many people as you can who are involved in companies and industries of interest to you, one route is to take a job – any job – inside a company that interests you, no matter how lowly the position may be. This is especially effective in notoriously hard-to-crack businesses, like publishing or film.

Beth Calabro wanted to get her start in show business. She targeted Miramax, the film studio. "Miramax gets tons of resumes every day," Calabro says. "Without a personal contact it's virtually impossible" to get inside the company. After a year and a half of trying, she landed a temporary job as a receptionist through a friend of her boyfriend.

Once at Miramax, Calabro didn't just sit and answer the phone. She got to know her co-workers. One person she spoke to happened to be a vice president at the company. The VP noted that Calabro was new – "it's a small company, so that kind of thing is obvious," she notes – and they soon began chatting about their favorite movies. When the VP needed an assistant, he remembered the young woman who shared his enthusiasm for movies and tapped Calabro for the position. Calabro advanced to become director of production and development.

Price Hicks, the director of education for the Academy of Arts and Sciences, says it doesn't really matter what your first job in the entertainment industry is because "there is no view of this business except inside the fortress. Once in, you can look around." In fact, Hicks says, the low rung on the ladder might be an ideal starting place. "The mailroom is the best place to work," she says. "You're in the nerve center where everything goes in and goes out. [Mailroom clerks] know everything that's going on. They see the mail. They see the memos. They see what's going on." The position allows you to compile the level of information needed to learn the ins and outs of the industry – if you understand the advantages it affords. At entertainment agencies, Hicks notes, mailroom workers often move up to become junior agents.

Your old job may lead to your new job

Needless to say, the days of golden watches for 50 years of loyal company service are past. The more cynical now advise you to treat each job you have as a finite contract. What this means is that your co-workers and supervisors have likely hopped from job to job and may be a valuable source of job information and leads. Have some discretion – don't ask your current boss for job leads if you're not prepared to pack up your desk – but don't hesitate to tap former and current co-workers, peers and bosses for information.

Erik Jorgensen, a group product planner at Microsoft, has moved companies twice in recent years. From Procter & Gamble he jumped to Dial, and from Dial, he moved to Microsoft. "In both cases, I switched through people I knew," he says. He had initially been approached by a headhunter to work for Dial. He turned an offer down, "but my old mentor at P&G who was running one of the divisions called, and said, 'Come to my group.' That changed my mind."

Totah, our headhunter who spurned the music industry, says asking bosses or former bosses for advice while searching for a job is a good idea, because they will be able to dispense valuable advice and references. "If you're talking to a boss about going to a competitor, it may be a problem, but the people who really care about you will want you to be happy."

Vault Profile: Erik Jorgensen

Erik Jorgensen got his first job after school the old-fashioned way – sort of. While getting his undergraduate degree from Stanford, he saw advertisements for brand management positions with Procter & Gamble – for business school students. Jorgensen applied and landed one of the choice positions anyway, one of about 10 assistant brand managers without an MBA hired by the consumer goods giant that year.

Jorgensen buddies up to his boss

Since then, it's the companies that have come looking for Jorgensen – often through people he knows. Jorgensen left Procter & Gamble for Dial after some convincing by his former mentor at P&G, who had already moved on to the soap giant. He then moved from Dial to Microsoft, getting pulled into the high tech industry by a former Disney person with whom he had worked on a co-promotional project (Liquid Dial and *The Lion King*, in case you were wondering).

Jorgensen, a 29-year-old Southern California native, attributes part of the relative ease with which he has found jobs in the consumer goods industry to to a "liquid" industry, with a strong headhunting network. However, developing relationships with mentors at places like P&G and Dial hasn't hurt.

"A lot of times I've been helped by a prior boss, or someone who was in my management chain," he says. "For me the preferred route to keeping in touch

Jorgensen profile, cont'd...

isn't formal. I just ask questions, or go to lunch with my people once a month. There's no formal commitment from anyone that they're going to play any ongoing role. If we're mutually comfortable, it's a pretty good way to go about it."

Jorgensen keeps in close touch not only with former mentors and bosses, but also former colleagues. In Washington, he's a part of a group of current and former Microsofties that meet every other month for dinner. As for old college friends, Jorgensen has season tickets for Stanford football games, and also goes to a couple of baseball and basketball games a year.

"Particularly in Stanford, the tailgaters at football games are pretty good events to keep up with each other," Jorgensen says, although he admits that the conversations aren't always pure catch-up. "People will talk business at these things, they'll compare notes on what one company or another is like."

Jorgensen is sitting pretty these days as a group product manager with software giant Microsoft, and isn't thinking too much about moving. "In the high tech industry, Microsoft's the only place to be," he says. Still, that doesn't mean people have stopped trying to find him jobs.

"I've gotten follow-up calls from people in companies after a Stanford football weekend: 'Hey you're at Microsoft, so-and-so gave me your name, would you be interested in talking to us?'"

By schmoozing, expanding your circle of contacts, and keeping in touch, you'll be keeping yourself in the job market whether you know it or not. When it does come time to find a new job, you'll have a vast variety of helpful folks to call upon. Price Hicks, the aforementioned education director for the Academy of Arts & Sciences, advises her former interns to "stay in touch" with former co-workers. "Read the trades," comments Hicks. "If you see the name of someone you know, drop a note, fax, e-mail, a card, whatever. Just stay in touch, and at the same time, give them an update on what you're doing. Even if you don't get a response, believe me, they'll remember you for it. You have to be nicely aggressive. You can never drop the ball in schmoozing for a job."

KEY CONCEPTS

- Tell everyone you're looking.
- Use alumni resources and internships.
- Keep in touch with former bosses and co-workers.
- Meet people informally through informational interviews — and don't ask for jobs directly.

America's Schmooziest Schools

1. **Brown University (Providence, RI)** – Hey, they've got a frat with an outdoor hot tub (at least last we checked). This is also the only college to be featured in *Vanity Fair* for its schmooziness. For these privileged kids, schmoozing is the only requirement.

2. **University of Southern California (Los Angeles, CA)** – The rich kid's party school in sunny California, where Saturdays in the fall for students and alums mean one big schmoozy, boozy parking lot.

3. **Morehouse and Spelman Colleges (Atlanta, GA)** – Students at these elite, historically black brother/sister colleges can count on a warm welcome from connected alums upon graduation. These include such schmoozefests as the annual New York City summer picnic for Morehouse and Spelman grads. The schmoozing, however, starts even before school does – alums pitch hard at hors d'oeurve-laden recruiting functions that feature proud endorsements from star graduates like Spike Lee.

4. **Princeton (Princeton, NJ)** – A school where you have to join a club to eat (sort of). You can't help but find a like-minded environment where most of the students dine at one of the school's cozy eating clubs. The Naked Olympics (sophomores run through the campus naked during the first snowfall) offers evidence that these Tigers don't suffer from shyness.

5. **Middlebury (Middlebury, VT)** – This bucolic Vermont school, located near the famed Killington ski resort, is home to one of higher education's strangest myths – that two out of three students marry

another Middlebury student. Although the myth has been debunked by some alumni research, it's an ongoing joke among students, and "No one seems to date, but everyone seems to marry," one confused student told *The New York Times.* We guess they learn to like each other on those long trips on the ski lift.

6. **Brigham Young University (Provo, UT)** – Not afraid of approaching strangers, these clean-cut men and women of God don't have a problem finding similarities with each other.

7. **Ohio State University (Columbus, OH)** – With more than 30,000 students, you've got to be able to find somebody to bond with.

8. **Parsons School of Design (New York, NY)** – Dahling, these couture college students have to know how to work a room. Alums include media darlings Donna Karan and Isaac Mizrahi.

9. **Texas A&M (College Station, TX)** – Y'all will wear big pieces of jewelry proudly proclaiming y'all's Aggie roots after graduating from this fiercely loyal Texas school, the better to encourage alum schmoozing.

10. **Amherst College (Amherst, MA)** – The insularity of "The College on the Hill" lends to its schmooziness. With only 400 people per class, everybody knows everybody at this prep school, old-boy member of "The Little Three."

CHAPTER 10

SCHMOOZING ON THE JOB

Sugar, it's good for you

Office politics are an inescapable fact of workaday life. Although the cream generally rises to the top, a little sugar never hurt either. Stanford Business School professor Thomas Harrell has found through a study of Stanford business school graduates that the only consistent predictor of success is not class background or intelligence, but verbal fluency — the ability to schmooze. Says Harrell, "If they like you, you'll move up." Ronald Deluga, a psychology professor at Bryant College in Rhode Island whose main interest is subordinate/managerial relationships in the workplace, states the case bluntly. "The idea is to get the boss to like you so you can cash in later in terms of promotions and desirable perks and all kinds of things," he says.

For this chapter, we went to the experts at schmoozing on the job and office politics — we went to the politicians. Let's not get carried away, though. Schmoozing can never replace competence. Believing you can charm your way to the top without talent or dedication is certainly more dangerous than believing that life is a strict meritocracy.

Competence is vital in any field — politics included. "The important thing initially, for someone participating in local politics for the first time, is to volunteer to assist in local races, and to be competent at it — because many individuals volunteer," says Tom Bucci, formerly the mayor of Bridgeport, Conn. "You want to be noticed, and you'll be noticed if you're doing it with a degree of competence. Your initial immersion in it is to volunteer, assist, and keep your eyes open to see how it's done." Jim, the onetime school board head in a medium-sized city, agrees with the work hard, wait-your-turn-and-get-noticed strategy: "If you try to be the boss, the chief right off the bat, you're going to have a lot of competition. Since everyone's looking for workers, it's easy to excel at that. It's also easy from there to sit back and see what the dynamics are." And Deluga, who makes a living studying job schmoozing, has found in his experiments that unsurprisingly, employees who perform best are liked best by their supervisors.

Schmoozing the big people

Finding a mentor within a company has always been an important part of the scramble up the career ladder. "Basically, you want to find out who's the rising star, and you want to make sure you're that person's boy," says Mark Hernandez, our aforementioned derivatives guru. But as our politicians' comments suggest, one of the dangers of politics is coming off as too eager and ambitious. Says Bucci, "You want to be noticed, but you realize you have to be viewed as in the background. Those already in positions of influence view you as a threat. You've got to spend a certain amount of time letting people understand that's the role you're going to play, and you're willing to play that role."

Vault Profile: Tom Bucci

When he was 37, Tom Bucci, Sr. became the Mayor of Bridgeport, the largest city in Connecticut. He had never held an elected office before. Although his two terms were marked by financial troubles largely inherited, Bucci doesn't seem troubled by his political experience. Although no longer actively involved in local politics outside of the occasional fundraiser, Democrat Bucci is still trying to help the little man, as an employment discrimination lawyer with the Bridgeport firm of Willinger & Bucci.

Bucci's the one in the middle

"I'm busy in my law practice, and it takes up a lot of time," Bucci says. "But having spent time away from my own children because of politics, I'm making up for it by spending time with my grandchildren. I've been given a second chance."

A native of Bridgeport, Bucci became involved in local politics fresh out of college. "It was an interest that I had that I've always had. I took time off from it, in the sense of going to law school (at the University of Connecticut in the early 1970s). I came back to Bridgeport and got involved in the campaigns in 1975."

Bridgeport at the time was ruled by a Democrat mayor and as such, Bucci says, no other Democrats were being groomed for leadership positions. When that administration was toppled by scandal, a vacuum was left in the party. Bucci ran for mayor in 1983, came in second in the primary, became more vocal in the press and at public gatherings like city council meetings, and in 1985 won his party's nomination and the city's top office.

Bucci profile, cont'd...

Among the things he learned on the job: how to appeal to voters as a person. "You improve tremendously at it — you have to project an air of confidence and be able to articulate your thoughts, and be likeable ... People want things personalized."

Bucci joined his firm as a partner after being defeated in the 1989 election. Although he wasn't able to spend as much time with his son and daughter as he would have liked because of obligations as a government figure, Bucci works side-by-side with his son, Tom, Jr., who is an attorney with the firm. Being mayor also certainly helped his law practice, but "as time has gone by, that initial benefit has decreased," Bucci says. "But the benefits of being mayor in the sense of developing a presence, being able to address issues, have remained."

More than anything else, Bucci appreciates his years at the head of his home city not because of whatever prestige he's gotten, or the presence he can project, but because of what he can receive. While some would say that legendary schmoozer Bill Clinton is a great politician because he listens so intently, Bucci believes he learned to listen more intently by being a politician.

"It's very important, especially with clients, because I'm better at listening. Not in a false sense. You just develop a sensitivity," Bucci tells us. "In my law practice, where I'm dealing for the most part with employees, I believe that sensitivity that I developed as mayor — dealing with neighborhood issues, meeting with people in their neighborhoods — has helped me a great deal."

In many cases, it's difficult to find a way to talk to higher-ups. "If you're just starting out on a job, you can't really just go and knock on the door," says consultant Granville Toogood about the problems of approaching higher-ups on the job. Toogood, who works with executives at major companies on their communications skills, is something of an expert on how best to take advantage of those potentially golden moments spent in an elevator with a supervisor, or a hallway — or even the bathroom. The main reason these moments are magical, he says, is that for a few seconds you can have a "conversation that basically makes you equals."

Do you just sit around and wait for your boss to step into the elevator you're on? You could, and it might work, but then again, it might never happen. Instead, conveniently arrange to bump into whoever you're planning on schmoozing, as we discussed in "Hey, Who's That?" That seems a little extreme, you might suggest. Not if you do it deftly and unobtrusively. "You could make it your business to be in the hall when the boss is in the hall," Toogood says. "We've seen 50 years of movies, where boy meets girl that way." And you can use it too, for your own platonic workplace situation.

Want another oblique way of schmoozing your bosses? "When supervisors bring their kids to work, I'm really nice to their kids," says Thomas Harrell. Where the kids go, the parents usually follow. Sound obvious? Not so. "Some people just do their work. They don't pay any attention," Thomas says.

But don't be so naïve as to think that the only way to get close to supervisors is through wholesome activities like playing with their kids or organizing the company picnic. This ain't the '50s. Mark Hernandez says he took up smoking in order to get in better with his supervisor. "It was a career move," he says about starting smoking. "I recommend any vice that matches the interests of the boss." Hernandez expounds: "This guy's in charge of 20 people. If you can get his personal attention twice a day for 10 minutes, that's a huge plus." Bad for lungs, good for career.

And don't assume that the best and only way to schmooze the higher-ups is to get cozy with your direct superior. Personal connections within a company or organization need not be limited to a single supervisor — schmooze as many as you have time and opportunity to. Consider the people in other departments to whom you might deliver reports, or from whom you pick up materials. Just make sure, if you're talking shop, that you don't give the impression of going over your boss's head or speak about confidential issues.

Also understand that the reasons for developing relationships with supervisors are not limited to promotions or landing plum projects. These people have been in your industry longer than you and know more people in it. If you plan to stay in the industry, but not the specific organization or company, they can still point you in the right direction. And regardless of whether you plan on staying in the same field, your supervisors still probably know more general career connections than you — maybe some of the people they know can help you. Hey, you never know.

What to say

Once you've figured out how to get a supervisor's attention, you need to figure out what to say to them. The key to approaching supervisors is finding the correct balance of chutzpah and modesty. Don't assume that they know what you're working on — or that they even know you — regardless of whether you've met before. Because of the pyramidal structures of large companies and organizations, supervisors often can't take the time to know about all the people working for them: You may remember your grade school bus driver, but he probably doesn't remember you.

J. Owen Todd, the former state judge in Boston who has a notoriously hard time remembering names, gives a simple but instructive tip about what he finds to be a smooth social move by young, whippersnapper lawyers. "They will say 'Oh, hi Judge, Sally Wren, we met at a case.' I think that's a very sophisticated thing to do," he says. "What they're saying is 'Hi, let me introduce myself, I'm not assuming that you would remember me,' and I think it's very graceful. And of course, I repay the favor, by saying, 'Of course I remember you.'"

Ready, Aim, Schmooze! Researching your targets

You should, of course, know who your supervisors are — and more. As we learned in "Who Do They Know?" and "Schmoozing 101," it pays to be prepared when schmoozing a specific target (we previously described Liddy Dole's intense preparation while schmoozing for the Red Cross). "You find this out by scuttlebutt, by asking what he or she does in their free time," Toogood says. Maybe the boss likes golf or volunteers with disadvantaged youth. If you have the chance to stroll by your boss's desk or cubicle, scour his working area to pick up clues.

"You can use any of these things as a fulcrum," says Toogood. "The point of the conversation is to let the boss know you're alive and well, and let your face be connected with your name." Toogood's point is important: it's often best to start talking with a non-business subject. This is where the lesson of being social first from "The Schmoozer's Mindset" comes into play. Easing into a relationship through non-work conversations keeps you from seeming too forward or calculating.

Eventually, of course, you want to impress supervisors with more than your quick wit and engaging personality. Here's where the lessons from "Schmoozing 101" kick in. Remember the rule of not asking directly for anything? It works in the office, too. Hernandez explains how he schmoozed a supervisor who pulled him along at a previous job: "I would tell him a lot about what I thought the opportunities were in this field, how I thought things were going, how I thought things could be doing better." The key to Hernandez's style — no excessive negativity about the performance of his group, and no direct reference to the issue of promotions or increased responsibility. He's just talking, thinks the supervisor, talking about work — and oh yeah, he's got a few ideas.

However, you should always be prepared to state your case succinctly. Toogood, who works with executives at major companies like GE, has developed an exercise he calls the "eight-second drill." The drill is designed to prepare executives for those occasions in which they are expecting a 40-minute product pitch, but are only given one minute. But it also applies to situations in which an up-and-comer finds himself or herself in a magical elevator moment that will most likely not be duplicated.

"You have to be prepared to start with the good stuff up front," Toogood explains. Toogood trains his clients to winnow down their message from three minutes to two minutes to one, to thirty seconds, and so on, down to eight seconds. His method operates on two simple principles. The first principle is the technique of getting the good stuff (maybe your ideas about where your department should be going) up front. The second principle? "There's nothing that you can't say in eight seconds if you have a gun up your nose," Toogood says.

Vault Profile: Granville Toogood

Granville Toogood makes his living by telling people how to talk their way to success. Through books and lectures, Toogood offers advice to career climbers on how to make the most of those potentially golden situations when they find themselves in the elevator with the boss.

"You can sidestep the problems of the career ladder by taking a social rather than business approach ... in an artificial social situation which you can create yourself can basically obviate the problems of hierarchy," Toogood tells Vault.

"Toogood" of a schmoozer

A Philadelphia native, Toogood graduated from the University of Pennsylvania in 1966. He worked as a reporter and writer for *Life* magazine, and then as a writer for ABC radio and the *Today Show* on NBC. Toogood got into his current line of business through (surprise) a personal connection. Starting in the 1970s, he says, a childhood friend began asking him to join a business offering consulting services to business executives. The friend, Lee Bowman, Jr., is the son of the late actor Lee Bowman, who, as Toogood explains, had many high-level business types asking him for help. "They needed my friend's father to help to show them how to do prepared readings without seeming stilted," Toogood says. Toogood left journalism for the consulting world, but it took a little bit of persuading from his longtime friend. "That was the product of a five-year discussion," he says about his career change. Still, once he made the switch, "I just never looked back."

Toogood profile, cont'd...

Toogood spends much of his time on the road these days, working with clients in Fortune 500 corporations such as General Electric, and speaking at business schools and employer associations. His interest in chance encounters in elevators comes from his emphasis on brevity and preparedness when advising executives. "The answer is to be prepared," Toogood says. "The answer is to anticipate the opportunity."

Polish those apples

Not only should you try to be good on the job, you should try to make your boss feel good. Ronald Deluga, the psychology professor who studies workplace relationships, performed a study that showed a "5 percent premium for those who flattered [over] those who didn't flatter at the same performance level," which he translates to explain that for those who flatter, "the boss likes you 5 percent more."

Deluga's study examined 152 pairs of managers and subordinates in a wide variety of work environments: "from health care to banking to blue collar types to high tech." Subordinates were first surveyed about the tactics they used to get in good with their bosses. Tactics fell into three basic categories, Deluga explains: flattery, opinion confirmation (the classic "yes man" approach), and doing favors. The supervisors were then surveyed about their opinions of their employees; job evaluations were also checked. Although all three forms of ingratiation were somewhat effective, "most effective was flattery by far," he tells us. "Five percent may not sound like a lot, but say you're working for a law firm or accounting firm that's really competitive. In a very competitive work environment, flattery may give an edge over a colleague or peer."

Vault Interview: Bob Bennett, Clinton's Superlawyer

If the newspapers and magazines define our language, then Robert S. Bennett's official title is surely "superlawyer." Rarely is Bennett referenced without the superlawyer moniker — and in recent years, Bennett has gotten a lot of media time. As former President Bill Clinton's lead lawyer in the Paula Jones sexual harassment case, Bennett was the only lawyer from his firm to deal with the press. Bennett was knocked by some in Washington for his handling of the case, but he shrugged the criticism off and won vindication when the case was dismissed in early 1998. (But Clinton later settled the suit for $850,000.)

Superlawyer? Superschmoozer

A native of Brooklyn, N.Y., Bob Bennett has always had a stiff upper lip. He and his younger brother Bill, the former Reagan education secretary and Bush drug czar, endured their parents' divorce and their mother's four subsequent marriages — one to a stepfather so rough that, as Bill Bennett told U.S. News & World Report, *"Bob slept with a baseball bat under his bed."*

A top-notch litigator with Skadden, Arps, Slate, Meagher & Flom, Bennett's other clients have included colorful individuals like former Cincinnati Reds owner Marge Schott and former Reagan Defense Secretary Caspar Weinberger. Bennett got his start clerking for a federal judge in Washington, D.C., after graduating from Harvard Law School. He worked as a federal prosecutor and for a large law firm before starting his own firm with several colleagues. That firm was then swallowed by legal giant Skadden, Arps. We talked to him about moving about in the rarefied D.C. air, mentoring young lawyers, and handling the media.

Bennett interview, cont'd...

Vault: When you were on your own with that 50-lawyer firm, how much did personal contact mean for you? You knew all these people from that initial larger firm?

Bennett: Yeah, well, I knew a lot of them.

Vault: And so basically the lawyers that you were working with you were friendly with?

Bennett: Oh yes.

Vault: And how did your contacts help you get business?

Bennett: Well, as a lawyer or any businessperson, you have to look at yourself as somebody carrying a big bag of seeds and wherever you go you throw the seeds out. A lot of them just get blown away, but some of them turn into flowering plants. But, you know, you get active in the community, you get active in bar affairs, you put on legal programs to tell people you're an expert in something.

Vault: Right.

Bennett: And you always answer your phone calls. (*Laughs*)

Vault: So how important do you think personal contacts are in the legal industry?

Bennett: They're important in everything: they're important in all business. People would rather do business with people they like. If you don't have the expertise to go along with it, they're not going to hire you, but it's important to have personal contacts. People don't hire you just because they know you, but if they know you, then they may be aware of your expertise.

And if they know you and like you and trust you and have confidence in you, than they would rather give you their business than someone else ... People like to deal with known quantities.

Vault: You're in a supercharged atmosphere in D.C. I was wondering how contacts with other lawyers work, how they work in D.C.

Bennett: It's important to know what you mean by contacts. You know if you have contacts, but if you're a fool or you don't know what you're doing, then those contacts are gonna hurt you: "I know him, he's a jerk." If, on the other hand, you have ability and expertise, and people have confidence in what you're doing, then those contacts are helpful.

People know who they're dealing with and they know about you. You know, if you develop a reputation for candor and honesty and straight-shooting then people will ask you for favors all the time.

Vault: What kind of favors do they ask you for?

<u>Bennett</u>: Oh, well you know, recommending people for jobs, recommending people for school, sometimes people get into difficulty and can't afford a lawyer and they call you and you offer to help them out.

Sometimes people are down on their luck and you help them in other ways ... People sometimes will call and say: "Will you bring me to the attention of so-and-so at such-and-such a place to get my foot in the door?" That kind of thing happens.

Vault: I'm sure associates look up to you a lot. Do you have any kind of mentor relationships?

<u>Bennett</u>: Oh yes. I mean I spend a lot of time with younger lawyers. I work with them and I hope they think I'm a good mentor.

Vault: Is it the kind of relationship found within Skadden or do you seek out people to take under your wing?

<u>Bennett</u>: Well, it just happens naturally because there are people in my group. I naturally take under my wing all of the young lawyers or most of them who are in my group.

Vault: Do you think the [media] respects you when you don't want to ... have a lot of publicity around certain issues?

<u>Bennett</u>: They do their job: I can't control them any more than they can control me. Should I have a situation where I want a lot of publicity, I have the ability to pull that off. Because of my relationships with members of the media, on the other hand, if I don't want to, then I don't pick up the phone. But I can't get members of the press to just write what I want them to.

Vault: But people sort of look to you for the sound bite, for that important kind of tidbit.

<u>Bennett</u>: Oh, yeah. I get a lot of calls from the media on some nights.

Deluga also asked both supervisors and subordinates to rate how much the employee engaged in ingratiating behavior in the relationship. He found a "remarkable agreement" in each person's assessment of how much flattering was going on, which he points to as a sign that bosses aren't fooled by flattery — they just like it. "They know we're doing it, they know they're being flattered, but they like it," he says "We like people to flatter us. It makes us feel good."

According to Jim, the former school board head in New England, schmoozing those with power (in his case, local party bosses), is not necessarily about being a yes man or telling a person with power how nice his haircut looks. Thinking back to when he was active in the school parent-teacher organization, Jim explains, "It's showing them respect when you're out in public," he says. "You make a big deal of introducing the mayor when he's in your area — or with a state representative, you say, 'He's doing big things.' A lot of this is what my parents taught me — treat people the way you expect to be treated — but a lot of times you have to be more animated or dramatic." Translated to the office atmosphere, that means publicly acknowledging your boss for the "valuable advice and guidance" given when making presentations to other departments.

Deluga, however, says that because of the stigma attached to kissing up, many of the people who took part in his survey noted that they usually do their flattering when they and the boss are alone together. Alternately, he says, "you tell someone else that you know will tell them. That seems to be especially effective, because it doesn't seem so ingratiating."

Hernandez agrees. He says that flattery can also provide a subtle way of getting the word out about what you've done. One thing he recommends is praising your boss in a memo that is really about you.

He or she will see it and send it around. Of course, people will see that it comes from you initially. "You're smart enough to compliment your boss in what you write up," Hernandez says. "He'll see his name attached and send it around."

Schmoozing the little people

The first thing to know about schmoozing the little people is to know that there are no little people on the job. Not only are assistants the gatekeepers to executives, and therefore powerful in their own right, but they often have an immense amount of insider knowledge about the organizations they work for. You think the president's secretary doesn't know what goes on in the Oval Office? Bob Woodward, the *Washington Post* reporter who along with Carl Bernstein broke story after story about the Watergate scandal during the Nixon administration, got some of his biggest breaks from an Administration secretary.

Because assistants often come into contact with a variety of employees in an organization, they usually know the lay of the land — they know whose calls get taken, which executives are buddy-buddy, who the rising stars are, and who's in the doghouse. Also, they are often the confidantes of their bosses and can put in a good word for an up-and-comer like you. Finally, you never know what assistants are capable of. A.J. Benza, the former gossip columnist for the *Daily News* in New York, says he often got gossip tips from celebrity assistants.

The first, and most obvious, rule when it comes to building relationships with assistants is to treat them as valued contacts and co-workers, starting with being open to their ideas and suggestions. Acknowledgements of these ideas mean more when made publicly.

Former Mayor Bucci says that he often used the technique of incorporating the ideas of those that he met on the campaign trail when appearing in debates and other public speaking engagements. "I would personalize that and say, 'Look, I was going door-to-door, and someone told me this, and I think we should think about it,'" he says. "You say 'Look, this had an impact on me.' It shows that you're not someone who has a monopoly on ideas, and that you're willing to listen."

Listening may provide you with some stellar ideas, but schmoozing assistants means not only listening to them, but showing that you're willing to listen. As former Mayor Bucci indicates, this can be done by publicly acknowledging good ideas. It can also be accomplished by giving evidence that you have pursued such ideas or questions. Jim, our former Connecticut school board head, says that good listening can mean doing a little legwork. "If I'm talking to somebody, and they're talking about an issue and I have no idea about the problem, I don't know what the answer is, I say, 'Gee, I wasn't aware of that, I don't know, let me write it down, and let me research it and I'll get back to you,'" he says. "It works every time." However, the local pol cautions,

CAUTION!

While trading info is a good way to build relationships, try not to succumb to the temptation to slag on your co-workers with anyone at work. As bad as it is to be rumored to have insulted a boss or that particularly standoffish mailroom clerk, it's even worse to have dissed someone who might be sitting at the next desk or lurking in the next cubicle. And as with supervisors, colleagues can be turned off by presumptuous employees. "The worst thing is coming in and acting like you know it all," says Tom Bucci, former mayor of Bridgeport. "There are those who come in and they already feel that they've spent their time in the trenches when they really haven't and a lot of resentment builds that way."

And don't spend too much time visibly schmoozing on the job. You've got work to do as well. John Schenck, the owner/chef of the hugely popular Clementine restaurant in New York City, tells us that he used to think that he'd have plenty of time to go greet his friends and other customers. But now he says, "If I go out on a visit, I imagine that people are saying, 'What is he doing here? Why isn't he working on my entrée?' You know, a lot of people aren't there to be glam, they're there to eat."

"The key to making that work, the most important part — if you want it to work in your behalf — is you get back to them. If you don't, it can backfire."

Of course, assistants, we need not remind you, don't stay that way forever — no one starts as executive vice president. And when what used to be the little people move up the career ladder to become big people, they remember who treated them like human beings and who treated them like flesh-based answering machines.

Schmoozing with your peers

They may be your competitors, they may be your friends. They may be both. In any case, your work peers — the co-workers at your level — are likely the people with whom you spend most of your waking hours. Spending time with co-workers should not be as difficult as it may be with supervisors. There's no need for ambushes in the elevators: simply grab a bite to eat for lunch with them, walk with them to the parking lot, go out for a drink after work. Although it is relatively easy to socialize with colleagues, we shouldn't take them for granted. As your peers move up within an organization or industry, this level of professional contacts becomes increasingly important.

How to win over your co-workers? Many of the basic schmoozing lessons apply. Take an interest in their lives. Familiarize yourself with their families and interests. If you see a photo on their desk, ask about it. If they always eat an intriguing avocado soup, try to get the recipe. Now that people are working upwards of 50 and 60 hours a week on a regular basis, it makes no sense to keep your work life completely separate from your other "life."

Trading information or simply giving information to colleagues — whether an insider tidbit about what happened at a meeting or the best Mexican restaurant near the office — is one way to build these collegial relationships. The most attractive form of knowledge, of course, is the secret. Our school board head notes that trading information with reporters is one of the easiest ways to build and gauge relationships. "Going off the record is building a sense of trust," he says. "When I'm doing that, I'm giving a vote of confidence in you because I'm sharing some information with you. It is intentionally saying, 'I'm building a relationship with you, I'm working with you.' It's all about building a relationship."

Always be generous with credit and available for help. Your crabbier co-workers might feel compelled to keep all the credit for major projects for themselves. This, of course, means that no one benefits from their projects and work but themselves — and eventually, no one will help them. You, on the other hand, will make sure that you generously thank others for their help, and pitch in on others' projects. You'll be known as someone who gives generously at work — and when you need help, you'll get it. Good schmoozers know that helping others is the same as helping themselves.

If you work in a large corporation divided into departments, one of the smartest schmoozing moves you can make is to join any kind of interdepartmental committee or club, whether it's the Charity Fun Run organizing committee or the African-American professionals society. These half-social, half-business organizations are fertile ground for meeting colleagues and schmoozing. Your new work friends will help you keep an ear to the ground for any shifts in the landscape of your workplace.

PARTYING OFFICIALLY

The office party is a queer animal. Is it office, or is it party? The best schmoozers will treat it as both. That means not relaxing office standards, while using it as the excellent schmoozing opportunity that parties inevitably are.

Just as at any party, you should take the opportunity to meet and mingle with people whom you might not get a chance to see otherwise. You can approach people and ask them what department they work in. Express interest — and perhaps you two can arrange to meet for lunch in the company cafeteria.

The office party is also an excellent chance to chat with CEOs and other executives that you might not normally encounter. Do your research — find out what they've done recently, what their hobbies are, how their unit is performing financially. That way, when you approach them, you'll have something to talk about — and maybe have the chance to mention a pet project of yours as well. The relative informality of parties makes it even easier to meet people of interest to you.

While there are a few "dos" at office parties, there are just as many "don'ts." First and foremost, don't drink too much. In fact, if you can help it, don't drink at all. You may wish to keep a drink in your left hand. This will both keep your right hand free to shake and prevent anyone from giving you another drink.

Your career can be negatively impacted by making a fool of yourself at office parties. "I've seen people make complete asses of themselves at office parties," says Ben, a former writer at Zagat's, the country's premier restaurant guide publisher. "At one big office bash, a senior editor got completely drunk. He ended up smoking pot with the editorial assistants. And then he tried to kiss one of them. It was so horrible that no one said anything, but he ended up leaving the company two months later." For every office party flirtation that has blossomed into lifelong love, there are 10 ill-advised passes (or worse, abortive trysts) that result.

Another consumption caution — eat slowly and thoroughly. Sloppily chowing your way through a plate of chicken wings is sure to appall co-workers and bosses alike. If you must drink, try not to drink and eat at the same time (if standing). Otherwise, seek out somewhere to sit.

Now go have (some) fun!

The whole wide world of colleagues

In the larger sense, your peers include people like you at other firms or organizations. Shemilla Subance, a sales representative at HKM, a New York production company, says she has about four or five close relationships with sales reps at competing companies. She considers these people friends and often goes out socially with them, but these friendships also help her out in her job. Subance says she will trade reels of the latest material produced by her company or a certain director her company works with to her friends for their reels. The reason? Knowledge. "You want to keep updated in this industry," she says. "You want to make sure that you have access and knowledge of all the commercials shot, or techniques that other directors use."

"Some people are ultra-competitive, and they completely feel that sharing information is a bad thing," Subance says. "The way I feel, sharing information is a good thing, that allows for better competition, for more creative ideas to be thrown around."

Industry peers have ample formal structures within which to schmooze. Instead of company picnics or cross-departmental committees, there are awards dinners and industry associations. "A lot of times you meet them through parties, functions, or award shows," Subance says about her fellow sales representatives. "You bump into different people, you might introduce yourself, let them know who you are. You might follow up with a phone conversation, to see if you can have lunch, or have a cup of coffee. Then you talk about the directors they have, exchange ideas about the industry, and then maybe you talk about trading reels."

One of the easiest ways to build contacts within an industry is to stay in touch with former colleagues. "A friend of mine left Microsoft five or six years ago to start a merchant bank," relates Bill Demas, a group product manager at the Washington-based software giant. Demas' friend often hosts showcase presentations so start-up high tech companies can strut their stuff for investors. "By attending some of these presentations, I can glean information from other different investors and really get an understanding of what a startup has to do to succeed, what operations it needs, what the cutting-edge technology is," says Demas, who, like most of us, reevaluates his career options every so often. "I'm happy at Microsoft, but you still must make every effort to understand what's going on in the industry, for your job, and to know what else is out there."

Literary agent Victoria Sanders says she will talk about editors with her close circle of agents. "I definitely have my group that I call my posse, or my cabal. There are three or four agents in that group that I not only consider great agents but my friends." She says she usually talks to her close circle of associates a couple times a day, often for strategic advice. "It's 'What do you think of this editor? What do you think of the pitch? How would you position this project? If I'm in [a bidding] auction, what can I do to tweak a little more out?'"

And of course, beyond merely providing advice, maintaining close contacts with peers outside your office can push you toward greater success. Says Sanders, "We absolutely pass projects to each other."

Vault Profile: Diana Pearson

One would think that a weekly newsmagazine with more than 21 million readers around the world wouldn't need a publicist. But that's not the case. As director of public affairs at TIME *magazine, Diana Pearson and her team work almost around the clock to publicize editorial exclusives and business initiatives through consumer- and trade-media outlets. Pearson is responsible for getting the word out that* TIME *is '"The World's Most Interesting Magazine." And she must be doing a pretty good job of it. In 2000* TIME *received several nods from major media players. Most notably, it was named "The Hottest Magazine" by* Adweek magazine *and one of five "Best Magazines of the Year" by* Advertising Age. TIME *was also a finalist for the much-coveted National Magazine Award for General Excellence from the American Society of Magazine Editors.*

Pearson also helped publicize TIME'*s 75th Anniversary Party at Radio City Music Hall in 1998, a "Celebration of Leadership" featuring then-President Bill Clinton and nearly 100* TIME *cover subjects. According to* The New York Times, *it was "without question, the party of the year."*

Prior to her stint at TIME, *Pearson was the communications director for* Newsweek *(1983-1997) and a reporter with Gannett's* Virgin Islands Daily News *and the Associated Press based in the Caribbean (1978-1982).*

As if promoting the largest newsweekly in the world weren't enough, Pearson is also the co-chairman of the public affairs and education committee of the National Multiple Sclerosis Society, where she also serves as a national board member.

Vault: How much of your success would you contribute to the art of the schmooze?

Pearson: All of it. Actually, no ... hard work, trying to follow through on the promises you make. I'm actually not even a pretender to the major leagues when it comes to schmoozing.

Pearson interview, cont'd...

Vault: Do you have your own brand/style of schmoozing?

Pearson: I'm genuinely interested in the person I'm talking to, more eager to learn about "you" than to make a point about "me."

Vault: Who do you think is a great schmoozer, someone who has taught you something about the art of the schmooze?

Pearson: One champion is Don Durgin, a former president of NBC News in the '70s, who is a vice chairman at *Newsweek*. He's 1,000 percent "there" in everything he does, in every conversation he has, and he's super-smart, a sharp observer with tremendous recall.

Vault: Any advice for wannabe schmoozers? What are some no-nos you'd advise potential schmoozers against?

Pearson: Know what you are talking about. Don't say anything bad about anyone unless you want to hear what you said repeated — about yourself.

Gossip is good

Of course, as we just learned from Sanders, and earlier from fundraiser Juliet Gumbs, some of the most important information traded between peers in the same industry, is about, well, other people. Explains Stephen Butler, a sociology professor at Earlham College in Indiana, "Academics is all backdoor. People want negative stuff backdoor because everyone writes positive stuff. Nobody writes negative recommendations, so you have to use your contacts to find out the real info on prospective candidates."

A.J. BENZA'S RULES OF GOSSIP

A.J. Benza, a former New York *Daily News* gossip columnist, offers his rules for gossip:

"I never wanted to mess around with people's sexual preferences. I never wanted to write about what was going on in someone's bedroom. As far as I'm concerned, that stuff to me was private. Someone's medical condition, I kept that out of the paper. There were plenty of times we knew about that long before the rest of the country knew. But beyond that, if a story is not going to ruin somebody's career, or ruin somebody's life, I tried to print it in a funny way, in a kind of way that people reading it over their coffee will kind of read it and go, 'Wow.'"

KEY CONCEPTS

- Schmooze everyone on the job, from the janitor to the CEO.
- Learn your boss's interests and schedule; position yourself accordingly.
- Gossip and flattery are useful vices.

America's Schmooziest Companies

Vault.com researches thousands of employers, through interviews and surveys of tens of thousands of employees, to find out about company culture and hiring practices. Here is Vault's exclusive list of the 10 schmooziest companies in the United States. For insider profiles on thousands of top employers go to **www.vault.com**.

1. General Mills

General Mills: I Do

The world's second-largest cereal maker, Minneapolis-based General Mills is also a marriage factory. According to an insider, interoffice romances are actually encouraged. "They have a lot of husbands and wives working here," she says. "The company thinks this helps keep you in Minneapolis. Otherwise, you'd rather leave the whole city, and then they'd lose you."

2. Merrill Lynch

Merrill Lynch: Dr. Jekyll and Mr. Hyde

Employees at Merrill Lynch, the top brokerage firm in the U.S., say that during the workday "a lot of bankers pretty much keep to themselves." But after hours, things change. One insider raves that "every Friday, there's a happy hour where everyone goes. It's a great meat market. Everyone's looking to pick someone up. Secretaries are looking for investment bankers to marry, and investment bankers are looking for secretaries for the weekend. It's fantastic."

3. Genentech, Inc.

Genentech: Go Back to School

"Basically my description in a nutshell would be that it's like a university atmosphere," says one employee about Genentech, the San Francisco-based biotech powerhouse. "It is more like a college campus than a company," says another. On Friday, the company has 'Ho-Ho's' – gatherings to mingle with co-workers and friends. These get-togethers, usually between 5:00 and 7:00 somewhere on campus, are well-loved by Genentech employees. One employee notes the presence of many "Genencouples."

4. CLEARY, GOTTLIEB, STEEN & HAMILTON

Cleary, Gottlieb, Steen & Hamilton: A Schmooze-a-thon

Unlike most elite New York city law firms, which are often described as "sweatshops," Cleary Gottlieb is described by insiders as "friendly" and "social." It also seems to be a schmoozer's paradise. "I schmooze with people constantly," one associate says. "I will think nothing of stopping by one of my friends' offices to schmooze for 20 to 30 minutes." We hear that associates on Thursdays will unofficially organize a social outing at a bar — generally in Soho or Tribeca. And on Fridays, the firm has a cocktail hour. "People here have tight social groups," a source says. "It's a social atmosphere."

5. BAIN & COMPANY

Bain: Life's a Kegger

Bain, an elite Boston-based consulting firm, is called a "very social" and "very fun" place by employees. "At the end of the day, at 9 or 10, someone will send an e-mail around asking if anyone wants to go out for dinner or drinks," an insider says. In addition, we are told, "every bay [seating area] gets social funds so they can have a kegger or whatever once in a while."

6. The Coca-Cola Company

Coca-Cola Company: Schmooze or Lose

Not the most social of environments, but one where making contacts within the company is an absolute must. "Coke is a very political place," says one former employee. "You will do well if you know the right people and make the right contacts." Says a current insider, "This is a club. It is an exclusive club. And you've got to know somebody not only to get in, but to move up."

7. ALLEN & COMPANY

Allen & Company: Schmooze with the Stars

As an investment banking firm to the heaviest of hitters in the high-tech and entertainment industries, Allen & Company hosts an annual schmoozefest in Sun Valley, Idaho, invitations to which are extremely difficult to get. With a cast of celebrities and business moguls including Bill Gates, Warren Buffett, Tom Brokaw, Barry Diller, and Oprah Winfrey, this star-studded shindig could rival any major Hollywood event. To be invited is to be a player.

8. CONDÉ NAST **Condé Nast: "A Bit More Glamorous"**

Stilettoes and tube tops are not a rare sight at the offices of this fashion magazine publishing company, where many employees seem to have stepped right out of the fashion magazines they produce. One notes that employees at Condé Nast are "just a bit more glamorous" than the rest of the "workers of the world." Writers and editors are on top of the "latest trends in fashion before they even become trends." With a swanky new cafeteria designed by none other than über-architect Frank Gehry of Guggenheim fame, the editorial assistants get to teeter in their Manolo Blahniks balancing $40 plastic trays in the midst of celebrity editors and publishers. Some also have the opportunity to travel in the "hippest European circles" and to meet the "up-and-coming geniuses in publishing, fashion and everything else." The company culture requires that employees "be in a certain frame of dress, mind and attitude." For those who cannot — or will not — conform to their colleagues' "chichi code," watch out: there's a reason they are sometimes called "Condé Nasties." Says one employee, "I have seen some nasty politics on occasion."

9. Charles Schwab **Charles Schwab: Nurturing Women**

This prominent brokerage firm offers networking and mentoring programs for women. Its goal is to nurture its female employees so it can promote from within. So far, nearly half of the firm's female officers were originally hired as managers or below.

10. hp HEWLETT® PACKARD **Hewlett-Packard: No Schadenfreude Here**

Yeah, the company throws an annual company picnic and two "beer blasts" each year and organizes basketball, volleyball and softball games, but that's not why we picked it. We chose H-P because its employees get along in a relaxed, open-door, team-oriented environment where job security and company loyalty aren't just memories of yesteryear.

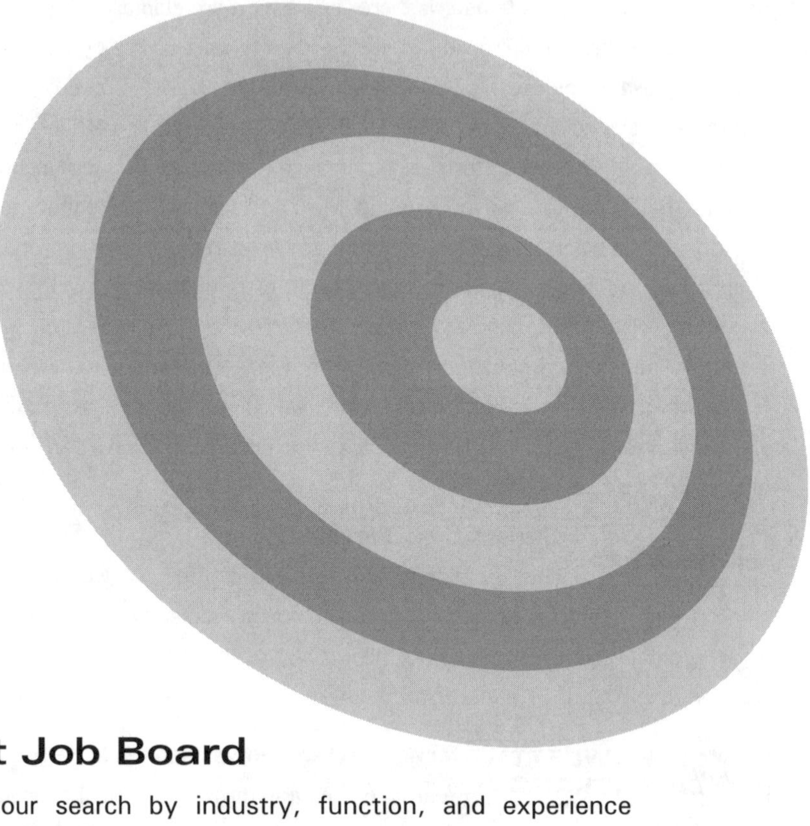

CHAPTER 11

YOU @ SCHMOOZING.COM

Why e-mail works

E-mail works because it's easy, it's fun, and it's unobtrusive. And because it's so easy to do, e-mail doesn't have the same emotional freight as making a phone call or sending a letter. It's easy to treat e-mail messages as casual, offhand notes — because most of them are. Best of all, there is no requirement that both parties be present at the same time. For all of these reasons, e-mail is a powerful schmoozing tool. Rob, a consultant at a major firm in California, who has successfully used e-mail to create business contacts, says he finds e-mail to be a graceful method of introducing himself to people. "It doesn't have the same effect as a cold call," he says. "It's not as time-intrusive, so people are more receptive."

For example, Rob once started an "e-mail dialogue" with an employee at a company he wanted to explore. "I got his e-mail address on the company web site," Rob confides. "He was responsible for an area at the company that I found interesting. He ended up putting me in touch with someone else at the firm and I interviewed there. It was a pretty effective way of getting in touch." That lead didn't end up working out, he says, because the position wasn't quite what he was looking for — but you get the picture.

E-mail works because it's less time-consuming then phone calls or handwritten letters. "For me, because I have friends from all over, e-mail has been a complete blessing," says Bill Demas, a group product manager with Microsoft. "If we sit and talk on the phone, it's more intimate and perhaps more informational, but I'm really dependent on e-mail to keep up with all my friends, because whether you write one or write 10, it takes up the same time." Demas, like most techno-savvy

FREE E-MAIL!!!

How do you get started on e-mail in the first place? The boom in Internet services means it's easier — and cheaper — than ever before. You can even get free e-mail for life from services like Juno and Hotmail, as well as search engines excite@home and Yahoo! But don't delay, for the Internet is a rich, barely tapped lode of information and human connections. Through the wonder of electronic connection, you may spend anywhere from a second to hours composing a message — and with a click of a mouse, it will wing its way anywhere (well, to any other computer in the world).

If you plan to do a lot of online schmoozing, it helps to have a stable e-mail account. AOL is the most popular online service, with plenty of bells and whistles to pave the way for uncertain users — but if you let your payments lapse for a month, wave bye-bye to that contact point. Many universities now give their alums permanent e-mail addresses, featuring the year of graduation.

There are literally hundreds of services that promise "free e-mail for life" (and that also allow you to keep the same address). A few of the best-known are:

www.juno.com
www.hotmail.com
www.yahoo.com
www.lycos.com
www.myownmail.com
(with a list of over 200 "vanity" e-mails to use)
www.eudoramail.com
www.mail.com

Free web-based e-mail is accessible from any web browser. Generally, you will have to watch an array of banner advertising while retrieving your messages. Don't complain. As with network TV, this is why you can use these services for nothing.

schmoozers, has contacts grouped by affiliation (for him, undergrad friends, business school friends, former colleagues at IBM) or location, in lists that are called "group aliases." "Most of my communication isn't done by alias — but if you need to blast something out, it's great," he says.

At the same time, e-mail is appealing. Though more and more people are going online every day, e-mail still has the feel of novelty to it. People who would never respond to an unsolicited phone call or letter will reply to an e-mail from a stranger, just because it's simple and fun. E-mail, in fact, is an ideal tool of the schmoozer for that very reason.

E-mail has the immediacy of a phone call and the content of a letter. If you're worried that you might get flustered on the phone, e-mail gives you the chance to compose your thoughts. "With e-mail," says Andrew Weinreich, the founder of the now-defunct online networking site sixdegrees.com, "you can compose your thoughts in a way you can't with a phone call. I've written memos where I say something like, 'Would you do this damn thing already?' and then I can take it back and say, 'Would you please.'" E-mail is also informal by nature, which has the advantage of putting you on the same level as the person you contact. George Bell, former chairman of Excite@Home, relates, "I can't remember the last e-mail I got that started 'Dear Mr. Bell.'"

"The great thing about e-mail is that it feels casual, but it's not," Weinreich says. "Have you ever been nervous about sending an e-mail message? Probably not. Have you ever been nervous about making a phone call? Probably. Yet you can reach someone just as easily with e-mail."

Schmoozing upwards via e-mail

The Internet is a blissfully informal medium — and a great boon for those who are a bit shy about approaching people in person. But e-mail can also be used to get in touch with people you don't know, including celebrities and executives. Bill Gates at Microsoft probably won't take your phone call, but it's said that the titan of Microsoft reads each and every one of his e-mails. And many higher-ups, such as CEOs, at other companies, won't publish their phone numbers, but list their e-mail addresses in company reports or web pages. Journalists often put their e-mail addresses at the end of their articles, practically begging for your correspondence.

This doesn't mean that you'll always get a response. You can e-mail the president at president@whitehouse.gov, and you'll get back an automated message. There are sites with supposed celebrity e-mail addresses, but even if these are real, you shouldn't expect these luminaries to rush to reply.

Some luminaries, on the other hand, are much easier to reach via e-mail. Unsurprisingly, you have the best bet of getting in touch with someone online if they are involved in the media or online businesses. These busy executives appreciate that e-mail is easy to keep track of and easier to control.

"I like e-mail," says Steve Kirsch, who founded search engine Infoseek and who now is CEO of software company Propel. "It's fast, and there's a record. You know who you sent an e-mail to. If someone calls me whom I don't know, they're likely to get my assistant and she'll call them back. E-mail I will reply to myself because it's faster that way. It's easier to reply to an e-mail, and you have control. If you return someone's call, you have to listen to them. E-mail is unidirectional."

But aren't these busy CEOs and executives constantly pestered by job seekers, fans and the merely curious? Much less so than you would expect. George Bell, former chairman of Excite@Home, says, "I only get about one or two cold e-mails a day. I try to respond to all my e-mail."

From the Prez to You

Subject: Re: Interview request for book on schmoozing
Date: Fri, 8 May 1998 14:20:25 -0400 (EDT)
From: **autoresponder@WhiteHouse.gov**

Thank you for writing to President Clinton via electronic mail. Since June 1993, the President has received over 2.8 million messages from people across the country and around the world. Online communication has become a tool to bring government and the people closer together.

Because so many of you write, the President cannot personally review each message, though he does receive samples of his incoming correspondence. The White House Correspondence staff helps him read and respond to the mail. All responses are mailed via the U.S. Postal Service. This is the only electronic message you will receive from whitehouse.gov. No other message purporting to be from the President or his staff with an address at whitehouse.gov is authentic. If you have received such a message, you have received a "spoof."

We appreciate your interest in the work of the Administration.

Sincerely,
Stephen K. Horn
Director, Presidential E-mail
The Office of Correspondence

Netiquette – Using e-mail right

When you're talking to someone in person, you can gauge their facial expressions and body language. On the phone, awkward pauses and shifts in tone can give you clues to how the person at the other end of the phone is reacting. But online, all you have to go on is your written words.

Because of this difference, you have to be careful with statements that can be misinterpreted — sarcasm, parody, etc. Because the Internet is a written medium, you can't always convey the nuances of jokes — howlers that you tell in the bar may come off flat in e-mail. Don't forward something to someone you don't know well. That parody of the State of the Union address that you find so undeniably hilarious may be either boring or deeply offensive to the person who receives it.

Is there a way to express emotion online in order to remove potential misinterpretation? In fact, there is, and you may have seen little "emoticons" littering your e-mails. The most common is :) (look at it sideways). Yes, it's a little smiley face, and meant to indicate that the comment preceding it is not to be taken seriously. An older version of the smiley is ‹g›, which stands for "grin." While some might say that the :) is infantile, or at least vaguely irritating, it does effectively puncture any tension that might otherwise ensue.

What e-mail isn't good for

E-mail's immediacy and amusement can make it seductive. Hence the phenomenon of "Internet addiction," where the obsessed spend up to 12 hours a day online. The gratification of having controlled "conversations" in real time, or of getting dozens of "letters" (e-mail) per day can be overwhelming, especially for the geographically or emotionally isolated. The lack of face-to-face, or at least voice-to-voice, contact, while it may embolden us, also gives e-mail communications a certain weightlessness.

George Bell, the former chairman and former CEO of Excite@Home, advises, "At some point, e-mail begins to fail as a way to deal with a problem. It's good for introductions or an exchange of proposals, but you really begin to lose the essence of a conversation after the first few e-mails. At some point, you need to go on the phone or meet in person."

Bell's right. While you can certainly find people and interact with them significantly via e-mail, at some point you're going to want to close the schmoozing deal by arranging a more immediate meeting. If you've entered into a viable e-mail conversation, suggest a meeting or a phone call after a few exchanges. That way, the essence of schmoozing is preserved.

How to find someone via e-mail

AOL subscribers (8 digits strong and growing) have the opportunity to use the service's "Member Directory" search. Not only can members look up someone by name, but also, through the "Advanced Search," they can look for people by profession or interest. All the major search engines also have "White Pages" sections, where you can search for someone by name or domain. Lycos has an especially interesting "celebrity e-mail search," which ostensibly supplies the e-mail addresses of well-known folks such as Madonna, Bill Gates and Quentin Tarantino.

Many schools have now put their alumni databases on the Web. Call up your university alumni or career office often, as these sites are almost always password-protected. Once inside, you'll be privy to the phone numbers and e-mail addresses of numerous alums; the grads themselves may be searchable by name, age, location or profession. This can be especially helpful for recent grads.

Vault Interview: George Bell, Former Chairman of Excite@Home

George Bell was a senior vice president at newspaper and magazine behemoth Times-Mirror, living in Long Island and commuting into Manhattan, when he got the cyberspace call from a little company called Architext in 1995. At the time, Bell was hardly idle — he was running the company's sporting magazines, including SKI, Field & Stream, Snowboard Life, Salt Water Sportsman *and* Yachting, *as well as overseeing the introduction of the Outdoor Life Network, a specialty cable channel. But Bell leapt at the chance. As he told Vault, "I figured the last time there was an opportunity to run a new form of media was the advent of cable 20 years ago, and I'd missed that." Today, Bell is the CEO of Upromise, a company that helps parents save money for their children's college education. Before that, he was the chairman and CEO of Excite@Home. We figured – who better to ask about schmoozing online?*

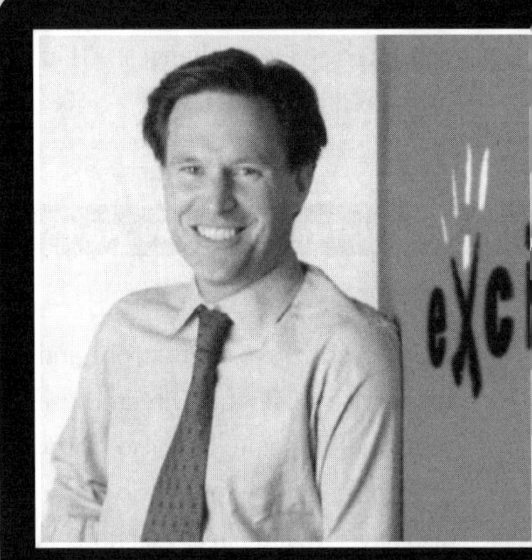

The Web's been good to George

Vault: How many e-mails do you get per day?

<u>Bell</u>: On the average, I get 125 e-mails per day. I get them from people we're doing business with, people who work for the company. I would say I only get one or two cold e-mails a day.

Vault: Do you get e-mail from friends and family?

Bell: Most of the people I used to call my friends don't call me that anymore. They don't bother to call me. I rarely get in touch with people. But e-mail has helped — it has made communication much more efficient. I can take home and deal with 20 to 30 e-mails at the end of the day. About once a week I'll get an e-mail from a friend of mine who I haven't spoken to in a while. I try to respond to all the e-mail I get.

Vault: Why do you keep your e-mail address publicly available, when you might not publish your phone number?

Bell: Because we work in the information business, our philosophy is behind keeping our e-mails available. We feel we should always be open to our customers and the public. That's our business. We don't encourage random e-mails or fan mail, but it doesn't upset us.

Vault: When did you first go online before becoming chairman of Excite?

Bell: Six months. I was using Eudora mail. I didn't spend a lot of time on the Web.

Vault: What use do you think people have for e-mail today?

Bell: I find that people in our culture are nowadays more willing to have certain conversations over e-mail. Certain conversations, I think, should be done in person, like meetings between managers, or personal criticism. E-mail shouldn't be a substitute for conversation, and it often is. It has reduced the value of diplomacy in our culture.

As far as entertainment value, it's a different story. It's fun, and you can, of course, get a sense of someone through their e-mails, just like you would through a series of short letters.

Vault: How are conversations over e-mail different?

Bell: E-mail is more casual, because it seems to be more in the spirit of the Web. Oftentimes, you find with cold proposals over e-mail, there are no introductions. It just launches into the pitch. That's fine with me. I don't remember the last time I got an e-mail that started "Dear Mr. Bell." I like my e-mail short and blunt.

Bell interview, cont'd...

And the ease is perfect. All I need to do is click reply and say, "No thanks." I'm not caught on the phone.

Vault: Are you friends with competitors?

Bell: There's still a lot of healthy competition between us and our competitors — Lycos, Yahoo. We're all 10 to 15 miles away from each other on the highway. Some people take competitiveness to different levels, and we figured that meeting each other face to face would probably alleviate some of the bad parts of that competition. So we met for a game of laser tag. It worked, and we all had a good time, winning wasn't the point. Anyway, we clobbered them. [Infoseek founder Steve] Kirsch got all dressed up in face paint, and it was very impressive, until he picked up a laser.

Many search companies that charge money for the use of their databases have web sites that pop up if you look for "people search" sites. There are numerous smaller people search sites which allow you to search for people with unconventional types of information, like a woman's first name and her birthday (in case a woman you know got married), and for specific types of people, like people with the same name as you, lost twins, and Koreans.

The "aliases" mentioned earlier by Bill Demas of Microsoft also are good sources of information that can be used to track people down. Poring over a list of e-mail addresses that are part of a friend's online mailing list is usually a good way to find info about people that you may have either lost track of or — for shame — forgotten.

Of course, there's always the possibility with aliases of inadvertently sending a message, meant only for the eyes of the person who sent you the e-mail, to the entire list, by reflexively clicking on "reply." Potentially embarrassing, yes — but not fatal, and also potentially rewarding. Those pals of your pals are excellent schmoozing material. Why not send a friendly message to the list, or a question — sort of an informal mailing list? Milo (not his real name), a graduate student at Harvard University, says, "I actually ended up dating someone whom I met because she accidentally replied to me on something I had forwarded to 40-odd people on an e-mail."

Instant messaging

There is no question that the advent of e-mail has created an important new means of schmoozing. But for some people, dashing off an e-mail and waiting for a response just isn't quick enough. Fortunately for those eager-to-schmooze souls, technology has provided a solution: instant messaging (IM). Once thought of as strictly a pastime for teenagers and pre-teens, instant messaging — a service enabling two parties to converse online in real time — has become a important tool of the adult schmoozer.

In a relatively short time, instant messaging has exploded in popularity. In fact, with about 30 million people in the U.S. alone using the technology at least once a week, the *Chicago Sun-Times* suggests that it may be "growing faster than any communications medium in history." America Online, provider of the most widely-used IM systems, carries about 750 million messages each day. Millions more fly back and forth in cyberspace courtesy of Microsoft, Yahoo! and others. And after a great deal of negotiations and infighting between the companies, the many systems should eventually all become compatible with one another, enabling any two people with Internet access to get in touch instantly.

Much like e-mail, IM has morphed into a common verb in the tech-savvy schmoozer's vernacular. Being successful at IM'ing is easier said than done, however. As with any form of schmoozing, it is important to understand the proper etiquette associated with the medium. Keep in mind that IM is different from e-mail in that the recipient does not have a choice of when to read a message. When you send an IM, a window automatically pops up on the recipient's computer screen. You never know when you may be sending a message at an inopportune moment for your schmoozee. Pop-up windows can be an annoying intrusion if he or she is trying to get work done — avoid IM'ing anyone who you suspect may be busy at work or with whom you would not feel comfortable interrupting in another setting. Furthermore, since your message will appear without notice, never send someone any racy or potentially inappropriate material without first establishing that he or she is alone and/or free to receive it. (Of course, if you are unsure of how your schmoozee will react to such material — even if he or she is free — don't send it at all.)

It is possible that your would-be conversation partner isn't that busy, but just does not feel like spending time IM'ing at that particular moment. Just as you wouldn't continually pester someone at a cocktail party who appears resistant to talk, do not bombard people with continual IMs in an effort to engage them. This also brings up an especially tricky aspect of instant messaging: if you receive a message but don't want to chat, what is the proper response? You don't want to seem rude by ignoring it, but you also don't want to waste your time. In this case the best course of action is to send a brief but polite response indicating that you don't have the time to chat at this moment. Let the sender know that you would like to touch base at a later time when you are free.

Given the usually conversational tone of instant messages — as well as their potential to interrupt their recipients — they are usually not the best way to approach people whom you don't already know well. This is especially true since most IM systems require users to adopt a screen name, which may make you initially unrecognizable even to your close friends. You may have grown up with someone, roomed with him in college, and married his sister, but if you send him a generic-sounding IM from "DarthVader7623" he probably won't reply and may resent the intrusion. To remedy this dilemma most instant messaging systems allow you to set up a list of contacts (known on AOL as a "Buddy List"), which in addition to helping you keep track of their screen names also notifies you of when they are online.

Again, while it is important to be careful how you use instant messaging, when done properly it can be an excellent way to schmooze. A number of schmoozing-friendly features, including file trading, news alerts, and voice chat, have recently been added to many IM systems. And instant messaging is not just for casual conversations with friends and other contacts either — large companies often use it to keep their employees in touch with one another on work-related issues. At the same time, do not become too reliant on IM'ing. Many researchers are worried that heavy users may become isolated and less competent socially. Remember, it may be quick and easy, but it can never replace real, in-person interaction.

Finding schmoozing circles online

Ah, those infamous chat rooms. These areas, which permit users to type messages to each other in real time, have a reputation as the haven of the feeble-minded, the horny, and the very young. When asked if he's ever used chat rooms, Steve Kirsch, founder of Infoseek tells us: "Yes, I have — to find out why people spend time there." One researcher estimates that 90 percent of chat rooms are useless or clogged with banal conversation.

Vault Profile: Andre Crump

Andre Crump, VP of product marketing for an Internet company that works for the construction and building industry in San Francisco, has taken the use of e-mail mailing lists one step further, by creating a successful electronic newsletter for the Bay Area alumni of the Kellogg Graduate School of Management.

Andre Crump: newsletter maven

"When you have an alumni organization from a top school, there's a lot of people who are really mobile," Crump says. "And then you have people from different classes that are spread across years. It's hard to really keep people in touch, other than in a social basis with a group of friends."

Crump started his first online newsletter in New Jersey, when he was working for AT&T. He noticed that there were some problems with haphazard e-mail forwarding among colleagues. For one, the same messages were often being forwarded to the same person from different people, clogging mailboxes. Also, there was nothing that marked forwarded mail as particularly appealing, so in forwarding an item, there was the risk that it would simply be deleted.

Crump set up a newsletter, which collected and then distributed e-mails sent to him. People began asking to be included in his mailing list, and forwarding information. "After six months, I had about 300 people," he says.

Crump has since moved his e-mail newsletters out West. The newsletter Crump has set up for Kellogg alumni allows people to post job openings at their companies and announce social events. It has even been used by headhunters (if they ask nicely enough) to look for candidates. While those uses have all worked out, "when it's really helpful is when people are looking for positions," Crump says. "I'll send them an e-mail asking if the posting helped, they'll say, 'Yeah, six people contacted me.' Almost everyone says, 'I got a call immediately.'"

Crump has posted information about his wife's job search three times. "We kept getting leads each time, and one lead has led to a job offer. She had to do a lot of follow-up, but she had her foot in the door. The offer came from a company to whom she had sent her resume numerous times, with no response. With the newsletter, she got an immediate response from someone who said, 'Yeah, my friend works in this department.'"

Crump's wife is not the only one to have landed a job through e-mail communication. He owes both his current and his last position in part to high-tech schmoozing. "When we moved out here, I sent an e-mail out to a number of former co-workers from Apple that said, 'Hey, we're back in the area, if you know of any positions let me know.'" Months later, someone called Crump to tell him about an open house that led to his current position. "This is not information I would have known about," he says of the open house.

While Crump allows that a certain amount of conscientiousness is necessary to run the newsletter, administering it is a relative hop, skip and a click for something so useful. Crump's e-mail program allows him to highlight portions of e-mails for categorization purposes.

"I take the old newsletter, delete the old information, pull up the different highlighted e-mails, and then I copy out all the relevant paragraphs ... in 30 minutes, it's out."

"They're content-free conversations," Kirsch says. "I'm sure there are some useful rooms, but I haven't found them yet. They are probably out there, and if I had the time I would check them out." Kirsh, however, isn't willing to bite the hand that feeds: "Remember," he says, "I do not speak for the company."

But Kirsch's comments about useful rooms should provide some incentive to at least explore the rooms. Many online services, such as AOL and Prodigy, run chat rooms with moderators, who keep the participants from lapsing into obscenity or "flaming" (insulting each other). Many web sites now have chat areas as well. Why not check some of them out? You've got nothing to lose but a few minutes.

Another option: mailing lists (sometimes called "listservs"). You can find a mailing list for just about everything that might interest you, from professional groups, to hobby lists. While some people may subscribe to the list "just to get e-mail," newsgroup subscribers say that lists often take on a life of their own. "Often," says Linda Malone, a New York computer programmer and a member of a mailing list, "these lists turn into virtual communities. I've made friends through these lists. I've met them face to face. People have found jobs and apartments — and it's not even that kind of a list. It's just that you interact with these people, and you get a sense of their personality." All you need to do is send a message to the listserv e-mail address, usually with the word "subscribe" in the subject line. Don't fret about having your mailbox overrun with e-mail messages — listservs are just as easy to abandon, or unsubscribe from.

Professional mailing lists are a great way to schmooze people online. The National Association for Black Journalists (NABJ) runs a mailing list for its members, who often discuss their places of employment, post new jobs, and help out people who are relocating. For more information, see www.nabj.org. And for those women interested in the possibilities offered by the Internet and World Wide Web, check out www.webgrrls.com. Webgrrls, an organization for women in new media, has chapters throughout America and the world and provides a free mailing list for both members and nonmembers, with job tips, apartment share leads, requests for advice, and invitations to industry parties and events. Want to find more mailing lists? Do a web search: two "lists of lists" to check out are www.liszt.com and www.internetdatabase.com. As long as you have interests, you'll be sure to find something that suits them.

SPAM, ANYONE?

Are high-level execs inundated with spam? Not as much as you'd think. Here's a sample of e-mails listed for us by Steve Kirsch, founder of Infoseek.

- Message from Reuters regarding a new product.
- Something from the brain, our adURL program.
- A message from my assistant regarding an e-mail I sent her.
- An unsolicited e-mail from someone who wants to do business with us.
- An e-mail from a contractor about something I asked him over the weekend.
- An opinion from a corporate lawyer on whether an idea I had is patentable.
- An e-mail sent to everyone in the company from a guy in the company forwarding an article that he thought was interesting.
- An e-mail confirming a meeting with the guy in charge of commerce.
- An e-mail from our corporate attorney about a police investigation that's going on.
- An e-mail from an engineer that works for me about creating a special index of web pages.
- A second e-mail from that same engineer about making purchases.

KEY CONCEPTS

- Understand the advantages of e-mail: it's quick, can reach many people at once, and is unobtrusive.
- Understand the disadvantages: you don't connect as well as you would face-to-face or even on the phone.
- People you think may not be reachable can often be contacted via e-mail.
- Check out listservs and chat rooms.
- Use e-mail and Web resources to track people down.

TV's Schmooziest Characters

1. **Norm Peterson,** *Cheers:* The epitome of the average guy, Norm was so empathetic that in one episode, when he cried after being forced to fire a colleague, he was designated as his company's hatchet man. So beloved that the whole bar greeted him when he entered.

2. **Benson Dubois,** *Benson:* An outsider in a bastion of white privilege, Benson schmoozed his way up the political ladder by bringing a sense of calm to the often-chaotic governor's mansion.

3. **Lucy Ricardo,** *I Love Lucy:* Schmoozed her way into Ricky's shows more than 30 times, plus a chocolate factory, a winery, and a beauty school. We all love Lucy!

4. **Sam the Butcher,** *The Brady Bunch:* The bunch's dark horse schmoozer, Sam flattered the Bradys and Alice by bringing flowers and slabs of steak.

5. **Captain Merrill Stubing,** *The Love Boat*: Always there as a sympathetic ear to virtual strangers about their own love lives, the captain was quite a player himself for an old bald guy. How many exes can you have?

6. **Michael Mancini,** *Melrose Place:* With that "Who me?" grin, the devilish Michael schmoozed his way out of a lot of jams with his smooth-talking.

7. **Brandon Walsh,** *Beverly Hills 90210*: Brandon went from dweeby twin of the laser-eyed Brenda to slick politico and romancer of the wan, yet lovely, Kelly.

8. **Bugs Bunny:** Bugs Bunny is the ultimate schmoozer — at least in the cartoon world. Despite his sassy stance and fondness for pranks, he's the most affable two-dimensional personality around. As lovable as other characters are, they lack Bugs' depth and wit. Bugs' nonchalant catchphrase "What's up Doc?" while casually munching on a carrot sums up his way with the world — he's interested in chatting, hanging out, seeing what's up. But he's also just detached enough to keep people hanging on his every word.

9. **The Fonz,** *Happy Days:* A core of schmoozy marshmallow in a tough leather-clad exterior, the Fonz is cool, doesn't let his friends down, and even makes conservative Mrs. C. love him.

10. **Bo, Luke, Daisy, and Uncle Jessie,** The Dukes of Hazard: The epitome of good-ol'-boys schmoozing. Yee-haw!

Other memorable TV schmoozers: Arnold, *Different Strokes;* Cliff Huxtable, *The Cosby Show;* Face, *The A-Team;* Captain Kirk, *Star Trek;* Sgt. Bilko, *Sgt. Bilko;* Mike Seaver, *Growing Pains.*

TV's Worst Schmoozers

1. **Archie Bunker,** *All In The Family:* Trapped in his prejudiced worldview, Archie never learned that to enjoy life, you need to open your mind.

2. **Jan Brady,** *The Brady Bunch:* Instead of cherishing her older sister's successes, she let schadenfreude get the best of her, wailing, "Marcia, Marcia, Marcia."

3. **Mr. Rogers,** *Mr. Rogers' Neighborhood:* All alone, talking to trains.

4. **Fred Flintstone,** *The Flintstones:* Loud, crass Fred can't be taken anywhere by Wilma — and he never gets away with anything, either.

5. **Blair Warner,** *Facts of Life:* Flaunting her wealth, the spoiled looker set up communication barriers to her classmates of lesser means.

6. **Eric Cartman,** *South Park:* With a foul mouth and a penchant for violence, this kid's got schmoozing all wrong. *South Park*'s Cartman has a volatile temper and is always getting into fights. (With his "French people piss me off" pronouncement, he's alienated an entire country of schmoozing possibilities.) He constantly makes fun of his classmates and declares his disdain for hippies. Some of his pleasantries in conversation are not quite fit to print in these pages.

7. **Fox Mulder,** *The X-Files*: Sat in the basement, watched porno, thought alien/governmental conspirators are after him. He had one friend, and even she thought he was a nut. Is it any wonder he's "missing" now?

8. **Ally McBeal,** *Ally McBeal*: Talk about lousy on-the-job schmoozing. Ally,

you're not the center of the universe, despite the fact that the show's named after you. Now put on some decent clothes and get back to work.

9 **Arnold Horshack,** *Welcome Back, Kotter:* With his own Brooklynese introduction, "Hellooooo. How're ya? I'm Arnold Horshack," few can forget this inner-city Sweathog from the popular '70s sitcom *Welcome Back, Kotter.* A class clown to the most annoying degree, he is best remembered as the one who always raised his hand shouting "Ooh! Ooh! Ooh!" when he thought he knew the answer to one of Mr. Kotter's questions. Unfortunately, Horshack was usually as clueless in the art of schmoozing as we was in the classroom.

10. **Murphy Brown,** *Murphy Brown:* She is smart, beautiful, and has a great job. So why is she so cranky?

Other bad, and sad TV schmoozers: George Costanza, *Seinfeld;* Monroe, *Too Close for Comfort;* Lenny and Squiggy, *Laverne & Shirley;* Ms. Hathaway, *The Beverly Hillbillies*; Barney Fife, *The Andy Griffith Show*

CHAPTER 12

THE SCHMOOZING MINORITY

It takes a community

Not part of the white male schmoozing bloc? Not a problem.

While being part of the so-called "majority" undoubtedly has its perks, being part of a smaller group or ethnicity can serve as a common link with others that can be used as its own schmoozing advantage. As minorities, the mutual struggles of ethnicity and race mean that a bond exists between you and another member of your group on first glance. "I went to the University of Colorado at Boulder, so when I run into Boulder alumni, there is already a pre-existing connection there," says Chin Yao, Chief of Corporate Relations/EVP Business Development for Click2Asia. "Similarly, when you run into someone who shares your heritage, it's easier to develop a relationship."

There are ample stories of how minority communities or communities of women have offered a helping hand to one of their own. In 1991, as CEO of Motown Records, Jheryl Busby presided over a business rich in history but poor in money. For help, Busby turned to his friend Charles Avant and asked him to mention his plight to Earl Graves, the well-connected publisher of *Black Enterprise* magazine.

By December Busby had a cover story on *Black Enterprise* and had been introduced to other important black businesspeople, such as Robert Johnson, the CEO of Black Entertainment Television. Johnson made a standing offer to buy out MCA, Motown's parent, thus easing the pressure on beleaguered Motown. Busby's new friends also helped him form a strategy to use Motown's platinum past to create theme cafés and TV specials. Motown's rejuvenation prompted PolyGram to buy the company – and Busby stayed on as CEO. "I had never before asked for a favor or advice," Busby told *Business Week* – but doing so sure helped him!

But don't assume that anyone of your race or religion will automatically befriend or assist you. Stephen Butler, a professor of sociology at Earlham College in Indiana, comments, "Particularly within the black community, our middle and professional class, though burgeoning, is still in its adolescence. So, as a community, we lack experience in the business world. There's not enough of us who can play the game." This lack of experience can create misconceptions or false expectations. Says Butler: "People think it's, 'I call and that's it, I get the job.' It's the modern McDonaldsian perspective. They want it fast, quick and easy like a Happy Meal."

There are many organizations grouped along ethnic or gender lines – fraternities and sororities, for example. But one of the easiest ways to meet people on an ethnic and/or gender basis is to join a business or trade association geared toward that purpose. Membership is open, and everyone is there to schmooze, mingle, and exchange opportunities and advice with the likewise-minded.

Why they're going to help you

Debbie Chase, former communications director for the National Association of Black Journalists (NABJ), says that black journalists "are very often isolated. They work at jobs where they are either the only black journalist, or one of very few," she says. Because of this, Chase says, "they are very interested in meeting others in their field."

Members of these organizations are normally part of an emerging professional class who want to strengthen the economic and professional base of their group. They are also out to create a professional community. For the lucky schmoozer, this means that members are already inclined to meet and mingle with others like them. "Our members are approachable," Chase says. "The more seasoned and well-known are willing to share insights and tips. Their goal is to build a core of teamwork, cooperation and support."

Melissa Wahl, who is National Director of the National Association of Female Executives (NAFE), the largest women's professional association in the country, gives similar reasons why women join the organization. "Women often feel they're at a disadvantage in the corporate world, out of the loop of the male old-boy network, which comprises the traditional power structure," she says. "In order to get an edge, our members use each other to gain connections and information."

Once inside

But once you join an organization like the NABJ or NAFE, how do you make contacts within the organization? The same way that you might contact an alum of your school, or a friend of your uncle's whom you don't know – that is, professionally and respectfully. "People tend to forget to contact an individual within the group in a respectful, businesslike manner," John Honaman, the executive director of the National Society of Hispanic MBAs (NSHMBA) says.

Honaman recommends sending a letter if you're trying to contact a specific person. This letter is the first impression you're going to make with this person you're trying to schmooze, so it should be professional and respectfully presentedz.

For those not looking to meet a specific person, minority organization conventions and other gatherings offer a buffet of tempting schmoozing options. Not only are such gatherings good for meeting people with pull, but they provide an opportunity to meet people from around the country who share your similar interests. This can be good for people looking to move, or those just looking to gain ties in another area.

Want to target your schmoozing at these gatherings? "Go through conference literature and research those people you want to meet at the convention," Honaman suggests. Speakers will be accessible – because they are *there* to meet people. And those looking for jobs, take note: savvy company recruiters attend the events to dig up talent. "I had one woman from Motorola call me to say she was very interested in the next conference because she wanted to find more Hispanics with the potential for leadership at her company," Honaman says.

The colorful info-highway

The rise in Internet technology has left its mark on all aspects of professional life, but particularly on finding contacts within minority communities. Feeling isolated from members of your community with similar interests and backgrounds? Turn to the borderless world of cyberspace.

Minority professional groups have begun taking advantage of the Web in various ways. The National Association of Black Journalists offers a free listserv newsgroup for members and non-members. Those that join the service are e-mailed every new message that hits the group. The list includes members and non-members, seasoned professionals, and interested neophytes. The interested may thus schmooze it up with a host of helpful professionals. Debbie Chase explains, "In the listserv, guests talk about everything, but particularly about events and job information, like what's going on in people's newsrooms."

What better way to (casually) flex your intellectual muscles before the powerful? What better way to reveal to potential employers your understanding of your industry and the issues that affect it? Through your online schmoozing pals, you also get to hear the dirt on what companies and employees are really like.

Some organizations take their Web use even further. Chin Yao's company, Click2Asia Network, uses its site "to build the Asian community online." The site offers access to English-language Asian newspapers and thus serves as a voice for the political issues of the Asian-American community. Click2Asia also provides free personal web pages and access to Classifieds 2000, a major job search engine.

FOREIGN SCHMOOZING

Building rapport can become more difficult across language or cultural barriers. For some, these barriers crop up quite often. Eduardo Blinder, chief of computing technology services for the United Nations, tells a story of miscommunication when he was working as a technology consultant for Pan Am Airlines. "I had a woman from Israel reporting to me, sort of a very hardheaded person," Blinder recalls. "Once she came to me with a chart that was very unclear, so I said, 'This is not very clear, it's not very intelligible.'" After making the comment, he realized that she thought he meant "intelligent." "She blew up, she thought I was insulting her." The woman was calmed down after "an hour or so," Blinder says. "It was not easy."

Blinder says a certain amount of miscommunication is a fact of life at the United Nations. "There is an overhead that the U.N. pays for being a multicultural organization," he says. "Things take a little longer time. Sometimes people aren't so quick to understand certain concepts." Part of the reason for the "overhead" costs of being multicultural, as Blinder explains it, is that the relationship between explicit statements and real meaning often varies from culture to culture. The Japanese, for example, he says, often will not want to tell people that something cannot be accomplished. One of Blinder's colleagues, he says, jokes that for the Japanese, "very difficult" means "no."

And miscommunications can happen even when the same language — albeit versions spoken on different sides of an ocean — is used. Remember Carl Bettag from "True Tales of Schmoozing Success," who found his job in part through traveling in England? Bettag offers the following subtle definitions: "In the U.K., if you say 'I don't care,' it's really rude. It's like saying 'I don't give a damn.' They say 'I don't mind.' "It's the same thing with 'quite.' In the U.S., it means very. There, it means 'kind of,'" Bettag says. "To say a meal is quite nice is no compliment."

As a start to overcoming language difficulties, Blinder says that when such a barrier pops up, one should use simple concepts, speak more slowly, be more direct, and repeat oneself. When it comes to the accidental stepping on toes that comes from cultural differences, Blinder offers some simple advice: "Just be yourself and be respectful of the differences. Don't make a face when they say your name and can't pronounce it — sometimes Americans do that." Also, Blinder emphasizes that situations involving different cultures are not the best time to whip out the joke bag. "Sometimes humor needs to be used with care. I tend to be a little ironic, and tend to use humor a lot," Blinder says. "But one needs to be very careful with that."

Vault Interview: Jane Pratt, Editor of Jane Magazine

Few people get TV shows in their own names, even fewer get magazines named after them, but Jane Pratt has gotten both. And just to prove that life isn't fair, she got both before she was 30.

Sweet, Sweet Jane

As the Editor-in-Chief of Sassy, *Pratt, then 24, redefined expectations of girls' magazines, with articles on issues such as homosexuality and premarital sex written in a style that put the readers in the prose as much as the subjects. The controversial and popular* Sassy *propelled Pratt into the spotlight, turning her into the new public voice of youth. In 1992 Pratt even nabbed her own talk show,* Jane, *the first talk show aimed specifically at high school girls. Although the show went the way of many talk shows of the period, Pratt has remained lodged in the consciousness of young female America starting her eponymous magazine,* Jane. *Vault caught up with Pratt in New York to talk about female schmoozing, the importance of mentorships, and the usefulness of electronic organizers.*

Vault: Do you think that women should have a different approach to building contacts than men?

Pratt: I definitely think that women are more inclined to help other women and to give them a shot. It's still harder for women in business in a lot of ways. It's important to me that I hire a lot of bright young women and create opportunities for women.

Pratt interview, cont'd...

Vault: How do you create opportunities for women?

Pratt: It's been really crucial to me that we have interns at my magazines. That's helped so much to keep me in touch and grounded – just in general. I did a book called *Beyond Beauty*. One of the people I featured was a girl that I just met. She knew *Sassy*, she was the coolest girl, and she was in New York, so I kind of took her under my wing. [Actress] Chloë Sevigny started out here, and now she's bigger than all of us.

Vault: What is the best way for young women to go about building contacts?

Pratt: The key is to seek out mentors. Every opportunity I've ever gotten was through a woman. Like, for example, Geri Laiborne was at Disney, the head of Nickelodeon. I've always been a huge admirer of hers, so I just called her and we talked and talked. It really helped me, because she's helped me with getting on E! to publicize *Jane*. She's also given me lots of terrific business advice.

Vault: Is it hard to find female mentors?

Pratt: I think women have progressed in my field, publishing. There are definitely more women in high-ranking positions. When I started right out of school at *McCall's* magazine in 1984, all the senior editors were white men. That has completely changed. I did find two really great women who helped me tremendously, they helped me in starting *Sassy*.

Vault: Do you act as a mentor to men as well?

Pratt: I love helping men and giving them a chance, too. I have a lot of male interns. But I feel particularly strong about helping out women. Pretty much anything I've done has been focused on women. I understand them better and I think that makes me better at my job.

Vault: What advice would you give to women struggling in a male-dominated field?

Pratt: I think you should be true to yourself and be confident in what you know. The best thing to do is just to hang on to what you know. You'll exude that confidence. I find it's good to pick something, like with *Sassy* and with everything else I've done, that I can be more expert at than any man. No matter what they say, you have that going for you. If you're an expert on something it will always give you more confidence and authority in your interactions with others.

Vault: Can someone get in touch with someone they have no business connection with?

Pratt: Sure. I prefer that they write a letter. If it's a smart letter, and I can see that they've done their homework and will take whatever advice I give them and run with it, sure, I'll talk to them. I get tons of mail, but not very much asking for career advice.

Vault: Do you ever get nervous about approaching people?

Pratt: Very, very rarely will I get shy. For the most part, I just push myself not to feel shy. The more people you meet, the less intimidated you will be with others. I meet a lot of people all the time so I have pretty much lost my caution around people.

Vault: In what ways do you take advantage of technology when you schmooze?

Pratt: I'm on the phone a lot, and I've gotten into e-mail a little bit. I'm pretty computer-phobic, but I do try. I have an electronic rolodex, which sucks. It is really bad. It loses numbers all the time. It loses numbers that I will never be able to get back again.

Vault: How do keep in touch with people?

Pratt: One year I did Christmas cards. And I try to jot down notes to people. I think it's great to be the one person who surprises people, sending notes, sending a free thing. People get a lot of freebies and free lunches in this business, but they don't send thank-you notes. For any little thing I get, I send a note. It really makes an impression on people, a good one. It's better to communicate with people when they don't expect it. I also get unexpected letters. Kathy Lee Gifford sent me a note. It was just cream colored with her name on it.

Vault: Any final advice?

Pratt: Here's a Hollywood trick – when you meet someone, tell them how nice it is to see them. That way, if you've met them before and don't remember it, you're still covered.

Got two X chromosomes?

Although it's no longer unusual to see female faces among the heads of the corporate world, the percentage of women in positions of power is still far from representative of the world we see when we leave the boardroom. While women are well-represented in some fields, such as publishing, advertising and health care, they are still a minority in most other professions. Because of this estrogen-deficient reality, women have begun creating organizations of their own to meet and schmooze.

Through its chapters across the country, the National Association of Female Executives (NAFE) offers regular opportunities to do exactly that. NAFE group meetings take place at least once a month and often are centered around speakers. However, time is usually set aside either before or after speeches for members to schmooze with each other, National Director Melissa Wahl says.

NAFE chooses to work through smaller groups because they prove to be more manageable – key for many women. "The smaller, local meetings demand less time away from work, and benefit many women because they don't take time away from family responsibilities," Wahl says.

"Smaller meetings also allow members to cater the groups to the needs of the area," she continues. In New York, NAFE members have formed groups that focus on different career fields, such as computing and finance; there is also a group in New York for lesbians in the business world. The Los Angeles area has a network group formed by and for African-American women.

Traveling members of NAFE who want to drop in on groups in other areas can find out about meetings from the organization's magazine or web site.

A RAINBOW OF SCHMOOZING ONLINE

AFRICAN-AMERICAN RESOURCES

Black Enterprise — www.blackenterprise.com
Billing itself as "The Virtual Desktop for African Americans," this site lists conferences and events and offers access to its black business directory and Kidpreneurs network.

Black Planet — www.blackplanet.com
An online community for the African diaspora that encourages its members to cultivate meaningful personal and professional relationships.

Everything Black — www.everythingblack.com
This site bills itself as "The place to find everything and anything black on the Net." Schmoozing specialties include links to events, business associations, network marketing, bulletin boards, chat rooms, personals, conferences, festivals, and civic organizations.

National Black MBA Association — www.nbmbaa.org
A comprehensive site with an array of links and offerings to help black professionals advance their careers.

ASIAN-AMERICAN RESOURCES

Asian Avenue — www.asianavenue.com
Provides access to information to help Asian Americans establish relationships and participate in community activities.

Asian Women in Business — www.awib.org
A vital networking resource for Asian women entrepreneurs that sponsors national business conferences and workshops.

National Association of Asian American Professionals — www.naaap.org
A site providing career resources and assistance for those in the Asian American community as well as Asian American university students.

(continued...)

(... A Rainbow of Scmoozing Online, continued)

WOMEN'S RESOURCES

Business Women's Network Interactive — www.bwni.com
The BWN aims to build more business for more women across more borders by disseminating information, providing access to education, and sponsoring business-related events.

Women in Technology International — www.witi.com
A site providing mentors and networking information for women interested in pursuing careers in technology.

Working Mother — www.workingmother.com
Affiliated with the print magazine of the same name, this businesswoman's network covers many topics of interest to career women, including networking.

HISPANIC RESOURCES

Hispanic Business — www.hispanicbusiness.com
Check out hispanicbusiness.com's calendar of business-related conferences and seminars throughout the U.S. and Puerto Rico. It also offers a comprehensive list of organizations and resources geared to Hispanic professionals.

iHispano — www.ihispano.com
A great resource for career event listings for Hispanics.

National Hispanic Corporate Achievers — www.hispanicachievers.com
Its member events are a great way to meet other Hispanic professionals. It also offers free listings in its Hispanic Business Owners Directory.

GAY AND LESBIAN RESOURCES

Gay Work — www.gaywork.com
Freelancers, consultants, small-business owners and the self-employed are invited to post their gay-friendly business services on the site. The site also offers a volunteer message board that provides opportunities to schmooze and do good at the same time.

(continued...)

(... A Rainbow of Scmoozing Online, continued)

MISCELLANEOUS

Diversity Inc. — www.diversityinc.com
Of interest are its online communities catering to African-Americans, Native Americans, Asian-Americans, gays/lesbians, Hispanics, people with disabilities, and women.

Green Thumb — www.experienceworks.org
A site dedicated to training and employment resources for older and disadvantaged workers.

IM Diversity — www.imdiversity.com
IM Diversity provides career and self-development information to all minorities, specifically African-Americans, Asian-Americans, Hispanics, Native Americans, and women.

Minorities Business Network — www.mbnglobal.com
A site for and about minority and women business owners, it hosts a calendar of events and links to professional organizations.

PEOPLE WITH DISABILITIES

National Business and Disability Council — www.business-disability.com
The site lists national conferences and seminars for disabled people in the workforce.

Work Support — www.worksupport.com
WorkSupport.com is a gateway for services and information about employing people with disabilities.

KEY CONCEPTS

- Ethnicity and gender are starting, not ending, points of schmoozing.
- Although minorities and women are predisposed to help those like themselves, you should still approach them as you would other tangential schmoozing contacts.
- Conventions = schmoozefests.
- The Web is an especially effective schmoozing platform for the schmoozing minority, because it can connect people with similar backgrounds and interests who may be separated geographically.

Willie Brown, Mayor of San Francisco

Willie Brown, the former Speaker of the California assembly and current mayor of San Francisco, was born and raised in the most segregated part of Texas by his grandmother. Although his trademark style, sterling dress, and bubbling charisma hide it quite well, Brown had to fight for everything he has gotten in life. At 10, he earned money by picking beans, cotton and watermelons. In high school, he shined shoes for quarters. As an undergraduate at San Francisco State University, he worked as a janitor on the side. And when he graduated from San Francisco's Hastings College of Law, Brown started his own practice because the major white-run law firms closed their doors to African-Americans.

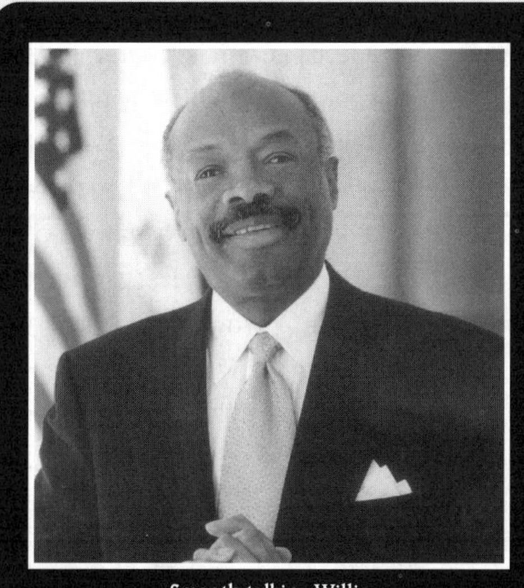

Smooth talking Willie

You might think that someone who has worked as hard as Brown in his early years would be super-directed. But Brown insisted to Vault.com in an exclusive interview that there was "no grand plan."

"I have always tried to make myself and keep myself in a position to take advantage of any opportunity, so I've always been a generalist in that sense of the word," Brown said.

Brown is able to position himself well because he is a legendary schmoozer. While in college and law school, he made important political contacts – specifically, the Democratic politico John Burton – and became active in the local chapter of the NAACP. He advises others who want to follow his footsteps to power to do the same.

Brown profile, cont'd...

"If I was a young person in the credentialing process, i.e., still in school, I would urge them as quickly as possible to complete their preparation, get credentialed, get it all behind you – whether it's a law degree, an MBA, or whatever it is, and do outstanding work," Brown said. "And at the same time, to the extent that time permits you to do so, become an intern, or a volunteer – get exposed at the highest level of the public policy world."

As a legislator in the California Assembly which he first joined in 1964, Brown gradually worked his way up the power hierarchy by doing small favors, one at a time, for other legislators. Brown did not limit his generosity to fellow Democrats; he courted Republicans just as vigorously. All this schmoozing paid off grandly for the lawyer-politician. In 1980, when Brown went for the speakership, he received support from GOP lawmakers to defeat a rival fellow Democrat. Brown remained as speaker for a record 14 years, earning a reputation for forging compromises and keeping his word. Brown resigned from the assembly to run for mayor of San Francisco in 1995. He won and now reigns over the Golden Gate city as its most popular mayor in recent history.

Said Brown about becoming mayor, "That happened out of circumstance when they took away my right to remain speaker; it became necessary if I was to stay in a public realm to find an alternative, more appropriate place, and lo and behold, the opportunity was there."

People talk about others, or themselves, as "being connected." It may sound hokey, but actually, we're all connected — interconnected, that is. Or we can be, if we schmooze often and well. When you look at people on the street, in your office, in your class, and around the dinner table, think about the stories, advice and interests they might be able to share with you. Think about all the stories you've just heard — those true tales of schmoozing success. Schmoozing can take you in unexpected directions.

Just keep in mind the basic building blocks of schmoozing:

- Have goals but no expectations. You should know what you want; just don't expect to get it from any person in particular.
- Be curious and open to new people. Get rid of the mental barriers that keep you from approaching people of different ages, backgrounds — and hairstyles.
- Be interested in everybody. The sincerity of your interest will attract others to you.
- Keep in touch and keep interesting people in your life. Meeting and schmoozing people is only the first step. To keep the process going, and to meet even more people, make sure you keep in touch in a timely and consistent way. The time you spend calling, writing and e-mailing will be returned to you tenfold in schmoozing fun and effectiveness.

Remember that schmoozing is more art than science. Don't be afraid to experiment with our suggestions. We've passed along advice from those we consider to be experts of the schmooze, as well as a host of little tips and quirky facts for troubleshooting areas — but no one can schmooze for you. Every schmoozing style is a bit different, and you'll find the one that works for you.

Most important, be brave. After all, how do you think we managed to find and talk to all those people anyway — both the celebrated and the lesser-known? Some we know personally. Others are friends of relatives, friends of friends, or friends of friends of friends — we asked around. Some we met in airports (honestly). And to reach a lot of the people we spoke with, we simply picked up the phone and called, or wrote, or e-mailed — and we asked for their advice. Just goes to show what you can do with a little schmoozing effort.

Enjoy the journey!

APPENDIX

ANSWERS: YOUR SCHMOOZING QUOTIENT

Answers: Test Your Schmoozing Quotient

Answers to questions on p. 21. Let's see how you scored.

1. Points **a)** 0 **b)** 1 **c)** 3 **d)** 1

   If you answered a), you've forgotten one of the tenets of schmoozing — always schmooze. Your fellow airline passenger is a captive schmoozing audience. As far as b) goes, there's nothing wrong with breaking the ice with humor, but saying something negative or frightening is ill-advised. c) is the best answer — you let your seatmate know who you are, and establish a personal connection. d) isn't a bad answer — you should certainly gauge the mood of your intended schmoozee — but schmoozing requires being proactive.

2. Points: **a)** 0 **b)** 3 **c)** 1 **d)** 3

   December holiday mailings are a perfect time to get in touch with people. Those who answered a) shame on you for letting a few stamps stand in your way! Contacting your friends and family is a good way to keep the lines of communications open — but better yet to touch base with everyone in your address book. But the savviest schmoozers know it's a good idea to stand out in the crowd. That's why b) is such a good answer — you can be sure your card will be appreciated and carefully read, because it will arrive at a time when people aren't getting much personal mail.

3. Points: **a)** 2 **b)** 0 **c)** 3 **d)** 1

   Don't scoff at answer a) — while you don't want to lean on nepotism, tapping your inner circle of family and friends is the first step to schmoozing your way to a job. Reading the want ads is relatively ineffective — only about a tenth of all jobs are filled through advertising, and you have little chance to learn more about the job itself. c) is the perfect schmoozing answer. The more people who know about your job search, the more people who can help you. While d) isn't a bad answer — it's better to contact someone in the field of your interest than to go through ads or random mailings — you would be better off targeting your resume mailings to someone you have already schmoozed.

4. Points: **a)** 0 **b)** 1 **c)** 0 **d)** 3

Schmoozing isn't the same thing as networking. It's off-putting to ask someone for their business card right off the bat. Would you hand your business card to someone who had barely said hello to you? It's not a bad idea to have the host of the party, as in b), introduce you to a guest of interest, but putting the onus on your host to make sure you get a job doesn't work. You will only make your host uncomfortable — so much so that you might not even get the introduction! Answer c) is merely weak. Good schmoozers are proactive. Make your own opening to talk to him, as in d) — the perfect way to start a conversation with anyone at a party.

5. Points: **a)** 3 **b)** 0 **c)** 1 **d)** 0

What are CEOs interested in? Their company and their employees. Answer a) is a gracious way to chat with the CEO. She will probably be interested in meeting a new employee and may even remember you afterwards. In fact, when you start at a new company, it's a good idea to introduce yourself to everyone you meet and tell them you're new. As you may suspect, b) is a cop-out and a waste of a great schmoozing opportunity. But c) and d) are not necessarily good openers either. For one, elevator rides tend to be short, meaning that you may not have time, as in c), to delve into the intricacies of the rupiah — and if the company lost some dough in the Asia crisis, she may not be especially thrilled at your choice of conversational topics. And d) goes over the line between schmoozing flattery and stomach-turning sucking up. You'll make an impression, all right — as a brown-noser.

6. Points: **a)** 1 **b)** either 3 or 0 **c)** 3 **d)** 0

Hey, there's nothing wrong with catching up with office friends at a party, as in answer a) — it's never a bad idea to schmooze those you know. But office events are also a great time to chat up others who you normally don't talk to. But be careful. Drinking as in d) is a dicey proposition. One drink may indeed help you "relax" — but be careful. Drinking also blunts the senses that you need to pick up schmoozing clues and cues, and increases the risk that you'll blabber drunkenly instead of listening carefully. This is your workplace, after all! Answer b) can be used for good or evil. On the one hand, if you approach your boss with solid examples of why you appreciate him and let him know what a fine mind he is, your flattery should go over very well. But be careful — if he knows you really think he's an idiot, your flattery will be counterproductive. Answer c) shows good schmoozing technique, what's called "host behavior." By greeting the new employee, who may be uncomfortable, and fetching her a beverage, you're helping her to adjust, and you'll have a chance to talk to her. (If you think you've got no reason to talk to a receptionist, think again — schmoozing everyone at the job is wise and makes your workday life that much more pleasant.)

7. Points: **a)** 2 **b)** 3 **c)** 0 **d)** 3

Not everyone is as pleasant as one might hope. Humor a) is one way to deal with unpleasant people. Even more deftly, you might choose to deliberately misinterpret the insult as a pleasant conversational gambit. With people who are truly hostile, your best bet is to smile and walk away, as in d). But responding rudely, as c) suggests, is a bad idea. It only reflects badly on you and impairs your schmoozing karma.

8. Points: **a)** 0 **b)** 1 **c)** 3 **d)** -1

Silly rabbit! How many times must we reiterate — don't decline opportunities to schmooze. You already have something in common with the people in the chat room — you're all fans of the output of the Brontë sisters. Now you have an opportunity to forge a further link with a person in your schmoozing circle. Answer a) avoids making a connection — no good. While b) could be construed as a continuation of the e-mail — and may inspire further discussion of hair — it's not really meeting the needs of the poster. Of course c) is the best answer. While your friend's sister may not be able to help, you'll have done a favor for someone, one of the first tenets of schmoozing. The absolute worst thing to do is openly insult someone (like in d). You lose points for this egregiously anti-schmoozing action!

9. Points: **a)** 1 **b)** 3 **c)** 0 **d)** 3

You shouldn't neglect your family in your schmoozing efforts. With answer a), you at least see your relatives, but waiting for family occasions is silly. If you're not still in elementary school, answer c) is even worse. Why let your parents run your social life? It doesn't matter all that much whether you speak once in a while as in b) or all the time, as in d) — as long as you make that proactive effort.

10. Give yourself 2 points for a), c) and g), 1 point for e) and f), and subtract a point for b) and h). The best schmoozers are open-minded, willing to mingle with people, and givers, not takers. A gift for conversational give-and-take also helps schmoozers. We aren't making a value judgment about being shy or facing the world with that certain bracing, cynical air — but being hesitant to meet others and doubtful about their good intentions hampers the art of schmoozing.

Score:

35 **Perfectly Schmoozy** The ultimate state of schmoozing is a rare and precious thing! We salute you.

28-34 **Schmoozing Savant** You've got what it takes to be an expert schmoozer — now get out there and practice. Further refine your schmoozing art.

20-27 **Schmoozing Apprentice** Not bad, but remember that schmoozing is a consistent process. Keep going.

10-20 **Clueless Schmoozer** You really want to schmooze — you just need to develop the right attitude. Smile, relax, and chat with the next person you see.

< 10 **Anti-Schmoozer** The recognition of anti-schmooziness is the first step to changing. Don't be daunted — just remember what we've told you and take it one step at a time.

ABOUT THE AUTHORS

Marcy Lerner: Marcy is Executive Editor at Vault. She graduated from the University of Virginia with a BA in history and holds an MA in history from Yale University.

Ed Shen: Ed is Exeuctive Producer at Vault. He graduated from Harvard University with a BA in English. Previously, he was a reporter with *The Advocate* of Stamford, CT.

Mark Oldman: Mark is a co-founder of Vault. He holds a BA and MA in English from Stanford University and a JD from Stanford Law School.

Hussam Hamadeh: Hussam is a co-founder of Vault. He holds a BA in economics from UCLA and a JD/MBA from the Wharton School of Business and the University of Pennsylvania Law School.

Samer Hamadeh: Samer is a co-founder of Vault. He graduated with a BS in chemistry and an MS in chemical engineering from Stanford University.

PHOTO CREDITS

The authors and publisher would like to thank the following for their permission to reproduce copyrighted material:

A.J. Benza: Ken Sax/E! Entertainment Television
Andre Crump
Andrew Weinreich: MacroView/Sixdegrees.com
Beth Calabro
Bob Bennett: Skadden, Arps, Slate, Meagher & Flom
Bridgett Bailee
Craig Enenstein
Erik Jorgensen
Fiona Smith: Paula Singer
George Bell: Excite Corporation
George Plimpton: Paris Review
Granville Toogood
J.D. Crouch
J. Owen Todd
Jane Pratt: Fairchild Corporation
Juliet Gumbs
Kaleil Isaza-Tuzman
Lara Rosenthal
Lois and Bud Ellison
Price Hicks: Academy of Television Arts & Sciences
Rob Nelson
Sidney Lipsey
Steve Kirsch: Infoseek
Susan Molinari: Craig Blankenhorn/CBS News
Tamara Totah
Tom Bucci
Tom Snyder: CBS Corp.
Vernon E. Jordan, Jr.:Akin, Gump, Strauss, Hauer & Feld, L.L.P.
Willie Brown: Dennis DeSilva

© 2000 VAULT.com Inc. "VAULT" is a registered trademark, and "VAULT.com" and "The truth is in the VAULT" are trademarks of VAULT.com Inc.